Goodbye Mike, Hello Judge

My Journey for Justice

Dear Michelle,
Warm regards
Myron H. Bright

As the longest serving member of the Eighth Circuit Court of Appeals, Judge Bright has had an extraordinary career, as distinguished as it has been long. His opinions, in cases great and small, reflect the depth of understanding, integrity, even handedness, and devotion to justice that characterize the best jurists. His autobiography opens a window onto a life that should be of interest to anyone who cares about the rule of law.
    David Wippman
    Dean, University of Minnesota Law School

For 46 years, Myron has reinforced day in and day out why he's such a top notch judge – his compassion, willingness to listen, and eagerness to debate in such a civil manner put him above the rest. But it's Myron's time dedicated to serving others outside the courtroom that makes him so special. A staunch advocate of equal rights and tolerance who is constantly seeking to stand up for those who can't always stand up for themselves, Myron's dedication to serving others has never waned. He's a model for others to seek to emulate and I'm incredibly fortunate to be able to call him my friend.
    Senator Heidi Heitkamp
    United States Senator (D-ND)

Few people in our world are outstanding jurists. And few people in the world are truly outstanding human beings. Judge Myron Bright is both. That's a rare combination.
    George A. Sinner
    Governor of North Dakota (1985-1992)

American legal legend Myron Bright has inspired generations of lawyers. His example of industry, dedication, and fairness is a model for jurists, attorneys and public servants everywhere. To have the exciting story of his life in this book is a treasure.
    Ronald L. Carlson
    Fuller E. Callaway Professor Emeritus,
    University of Georgia School of Law, author, and lecturer

A remarkable lawyer with a remarkable career, Judge Bright has helped to move federal law forward in noteworthy cases involving environmental law, employment discrimination, evidence, and criminal law. Above all else, though, Judge Bright's decisions have been informed by his genuine compassion for people. He is a judge who cares, and cares a great deal.
Kathryn R.L. Rand
Dean & Floyd B. Sperry Professor of Law,
University of North Dakota School of Law

Over the years Judge Myron Bright has built an extraordinarily strong and great reputation for his excellent legal decisions and his love of the law. The country has benefited greatly from his energy, longevity, and willingness to continue his excellent service as a jurist and teacher. I am proud to call him a friend and appreciate the friendship between our families.
Mark Andrews
Former United States Senator (R-ND)

Judge Bright has been a great lawyer, a great jurist and a great teacher. His attainments in those roles largely derive from the fact that he is a great human being. Over 75 years of knowing Bright, I have not met another man who so combines keen intellect and broad vision with compassion and concern for his fellow men.
David R Brink
Past President of the American Bar Association, former senior partner of Dorsey and Whitney LLP, Minneapolis, Minnesota

Judge Bright and I were introduced through a mutual friend and I am so thankful for that introduction. Some may consider it "odd" we have become friends. It may be his interest in sports and my interest in law that drew us together. I admire and respect him and truly enjoy every opportunity to visit. His vision, balance, wisdom, frankness, truthfulness and sense of humor are venerable qualities and I am honored to one of his many friends.
Amy Ruley
Head Coach, North Dakota State University Women's Basketball (1979-2008), Senior Associate Athletic Director, North Dakota State University

Judge Bright has the unique ability to be serious and humorous at the same time and of course this characteristic enables a serious conversation with no hostility. This personality has served Myron well in his personal and professional career. Myron is unique!

    William C. Marcil Sr.
    Chairman, Forum Communications Company

Myron Bright is a great judge who cares not only about the development of the law, but its impact on the people whose lives are affected. He is also a great storyteller. His recounting of his extraordinary life contributes immensely to our understanding of law, politics and society over the last century.

    Stephen B. Bright
    President and Senior Counsel, Southern Center for Human Rights
    Visiting Lecturer in Law, Yale Law School

With his boundless wit, energy, and enthusiasm, Judge Bright has made it his life's work to promote liberty and justice for all, with a sharp sensitivity for the abused, the victim of discrimination, the wrongly accused, and the unfairly sentenced. His unbounded enthusiasm for life and the law was and is even today infectious. He is an inspiration. I feel very proud to call Judge Bright my teacher and friend.

    Rebecca S. Thiem
    Law Clerk to Judge Bright (1980-81)
    Partner, Zuger Kirmis & Smith

Judge Bright personifies justice and fairness. He's also a man who is devoted to his family, friends, and faith. If you're lucky enough to meet Judge Bright, you never forget him and his enthusiasm for life.

    Jim Shaw
    Former KVRR-TV News Director

Judge Bright has continued into adulthood in his conversations with those of any age with such clarity and truthfulness that he has struck his many friends as a unique Saint of Clarity-Truth.

    E. Barrett Prettyman, Jr.
    Of Counsel, Hogan Lovells
    Successive law clerk to United States Supreme Court Justices Jackson, Frankfurter, and Harlan

Goodbye Mike, Hello Judge

My Journey for Justice

Myron H. Bright

Published by the Institute for Regional Studies Press
North Dakota State University
Dept. 2360, P.O. Box 6050, Fargo, ND 58108-6050.
www.ndsu.edu/ahss/ndirs

Goodbye Mike, Hello Judge: My Journey for Justice
By Myron H. Bright

Copyright ©2014 by the Institute for Regional Studies Press, North Dakota State University, Fargo. All rights reserved.

Book design by Deb Tanner.

International Standard Book Number: 9780-911042-78-853000
Library of Congress Control Number: 2014955187
Printed in the United States.

I dedicate this book to my great wife Frances (Fritzie) Bright. We were married almost 54 years until her death (1946-2000). Without her persuasive efforts, I would not be a judge.

Contents

Editor's Perspective i
Introduction v

Section One
Chapter 1: The Bright Family 1
Chapter 2: Law School Daze 11
Chapter 3: Private to Sergeant to Commission 18
Chapter 4: Officer and a Gentleman in the USA — and En Route
  to India 23
Chapter 5: Military Duties 32
Chapter 6: My Return 36
Chapter 7: Last Test and First Job 40
Chapter 8: New Lawyer — Fargo, Here I Come 44
Chapter 9: On Being a Trial Lawyer 51

Section Two
Chapter 10: Politics — the Beginning 61
Chapter 11: First Time I Saw Quentin — Beginning of a Friendship 63
Chapter 12: Nomination and Election to Congress — 1958 65
Chapter 13: What to Do After the Election 69
Chapter 14: Quentin Runs for Senate, Guy for Governor,
  JFK for President 72
Chapter 15: Birthday Bash With JFK Boosts Burdick 78
Chapter 16: Vignettes 88
Chapter 17: After the Ball and Burdick Benefit of '64 94
Chapter 18: My Time is Your Time — Your Time is My Time
  (Rudy Valley, 1929) 101

Section Three
Chapter 19: The Judgeship 103
Chapter 20: RFK and the Bright Family 108
Chapter 21: Appointment and Confirmation — Meeting With
  President Lyndon Baines Johnson 112
Chapter 22: My Inauguration 120

Section Four

Chapter 23: Stand Up and Be Counted — Acceptance, Rejection, Vindication ... 123
Chapter 24: Woosley: Justice Will Be Done — I'll Find a Way ... 126
Chapter 25: Reserve Mining — Jobs v. Environment ... 129
Chapter 26: Helm Case: Judiciary Anarchy — Make the Most of It! ... 133
Chapter 27: Green v. McDonnell-Douglas: Not Any Old Excuse Will Do — A Seminal Case ... 137
Chapter 28: Unfinished Business — Sentencing Appeals ... 142
Chapter 29: My Sentencing Philosophy ... 147
Chapter 30: Dana Deegan — Reservation Injustice ... 153
Chapter 31: James Dean Walker — Justice, Finally ... 161
Chapter 32: Piper Kidnapping — Do What in Your Heart and Mind is Right ... 168
Chapter 33: Looking Back ... 171

Acknowledgments ... 175
Appendix ... 177
Notes ... 181
Index ... 182

Editor's Perspective

Federal Judge Myron "Mike" Bright is the son of Jewish immigrants from Russia living in a mining community on northern Minnesota's Iron Range. He experienced ethnic and religious discrimination himself in that setting, and again when he began his professional career. It was also something he saw directed toward various minority persons. His legal perspective and judicial decisions have incorporated and reflected that background and his high regard for all people regardless of their ethnic, social, economic status or color. He has received national recognition and significant awards for his judicial life.

Still working at age 95, Judge Bright is looking back on a legacy of not only fighting for justice, but advocating, often as a lone voice, against injustice. He is the longest-serving federal appellate judge in the history of the Eighth Circuit and presently is the most senior federal circuit judge in the country. His legal and judicial career has been driven by his compassion for individuals who have been treated unfairly—including a Native American woman who herself suffered abuse her entire life before being sentenced to ten years and one month in prison through the federal court system while a Caucasian college student received no jail time from a state court for a similar offense. The conduct in both cases was permitting a newborn baby to die in the first 24 hours of birth, a crime referred to as neonaticide.

Among other memorable and meaningful cases, Judge Bright stood up for a "trouble-maker" black laid-off employee who alleged that an employer discriminated against him in a rehiring process, for an Arkansas man who was unjustly convicted before a prejudiced state judge in the shooting of a law enforcement officer during a police chase, for two men unfairly convicted in the famous Minnesota case involving the kidnapping for a million-dollar ransom of Virginia Piper, and judicial relief from a heavy prison sentence for a young man who conscientiously objected to military service in the unpopular Vietnam War. Judge Bright also found a way to save jobs while still protecting the environment in a landmark pollution case in which Reserve Mining Company in northern Minnesota dumped iron ore refuse into beautiful Lake Superior, and greatly reduced sentence for a South Dakota petty criminal who had been too harshly punished by life imprisonment without parole. He has served as a judge in more than 6,500 cases, in the Eighth Circuit and other circuits around the country.

Prior to his judicial appointment in 1968 by President Lyndon Johnson, Myron Bright was engaged in North Dakota politics and, more than any other person, was responsible for the election to the U.S. Congress and Senate of a man — Quentin Burdick — who, in his time, may have been conservative North Dakota's progressive equivalent of Minnesota's Hubert Humphrey and Walter Mondale. Chairing a political party in North Dakota's largest county, Myron Bright was also instrumental in the election of William L. Guy, the longest-serving governor in North Dakota history. In his political work, he became friends with John F. Kennedy and Robert Kennedy.

Burdick nominated Bright for the federal bench over his own brother, Eugene Burdick, who was nominated by a Republican senator, Milton Young. White House politics trumped the Justice Department and resulted in the appointment of Burdick's man Bright over a South Dakota judge favored by Sen. George McGovern. In addition to his personal behind-the-scenes perspective on Lyndon Johnson, Bright also provides stories of his experiences with political statesmen, including those two Kennedys, Harry Truman and Humphrey.

Although he was prohibited from active political involvement once he became a federal judge, Myron Bright did play a role in the appointment of the first woman from North Dakota to the U.S. Senate, Senator Burdick's widow, Jocelyn Burdick. And Fritzie, Bright's late wife, was a political partner of Myron Bright until his appointment as a judge.

In addition to his important judicial rulings and writings, Judge Bright's personal stories include his experiences growing up in a northern

Minnesota ethnic melting pot, his overseas military service in World War II, lessons learned inside and outside the classrooms and books at the University of Minnesota Law School, and developing into an accomplished attorney with the largest law firm in North Dakota.

Myron Bright continues to serve the U.S. Court of Appeals for the Eighth Circuit, which includes the seven states of Minnesota, North Dakota, South Dakota, Iowa, Nebraska, Missouri and Arkansas. The University of Minnesota Press, in 2007, published *Establishing Justice in Middle America: A History of the United States Court of Appeals for the Eighth Circuit*. The Eighth Circuit Court has ruled on cases that impact some of the most significant issues in American history, and Judge Bright has provided the heart for many of those rulings through his influence on the opinion-making process, his written opinions, and his passionate oral and written dissents. Though still often the minority voice, he continues to speak out loudly on issues he cares deeply about, including a "broken and unfair" system of sentencing in federal courts.

Judge Bright has been preparing himself to produce this important memoir longer than many of us have been alive. His ultimate process involved writing in longhand on yellow legal tablets and recording his dictation. He hired a professional transcriber for word processing and was helped throughout this endeavor by his longtime assistant, Lana Schultz. Serving as Judge Bright's personal editor, I have relished the opportunity to guide him in determining structure and content for this memoir — my most significant contribution has been helping him shape this into a publishable form with appeal to a broad audience. I'm honored to have had this role in helping get an important story told.

Judge Bright opens and sets up to share his life story with an insider account of when he and Fritzie visited President Lyndon Johnson in the White House to discuss the federal appeals court appointment. He and Fritzie chronicled and preserved the details and dialogue of that experience immediately upon their return to Fargo in 1968. Other quoted conversations included in this memoir have been gathered from published sources or reconstructed from Judge Bright's sharp memory, prompted by notes, correspondence, newspaper articles and other documents. What you will read is written by Judge Bright. These are his words. Indeed, he has lived a meaningful life — about that there is no dissent.

Bob Jansen, MFA
Editor for Judge Bright

Goodbye Mike, Hello Judge: My Journey for Justice

Introduction

The date: May 8, 1968.

The place: Old U.S. Senate Office Building, Washington, D.C., office of Senator Quentin N. Burdick, D-North Dakota.

The persons: Myron H. Bright, also as known as Mike, a forty-nine year old lawyer from Fargo. He is accompanied by his wife, Frances Bright, better known as Fritzie. Myron is there to be confirmed by the United States Senate as a circuit judge for the U.S. Court of Appeals for the Eighth Circuit. They are in Burdick's office in the Old Senate Office Building.

In addition to attending a hearing before a subcommittee of the Senate Judiciary Committee, Myron and Fritzie have an appointment to see Lyndon Baines Johnson, the thirty-sixth president of these United States.

Myron speaks: "Fritzie, let's get a move on. It's 12:20. Senator Burdick has arranged for the three of us to meet the president at 12:45."

Myron grabs Fritzie by the arm and down the hallway and steps they run. As they leave his office, Quentin shouts: "I'll catch up with you at the White House. I've got to meet some Farmers Union people from Jamestown in a few minutes."

Myron and Fritzie look up and down the streets bordering the old Senate Office Building. Strangely for the District, no cab can be seen. After they check the adjoining streets, a taxicab finally appeared.

Myron hails the cab, walking right into the middle of the street. The vehicle rattles as it pulls up to the waiting passengers. Myron shakes his head. It's a rickety rattletrap.

What to do? No other taxis were in sight. So Myron and Fritzie climb into the back seat.

"Take us to the White House." Off the cab rattles.

Nearing the White House, Myron and Fritzie notice many guards patrolling the streets and the entryways to the president's house. The time is the height of the Vietnam War.

The cab stops near the southwest gate. A tall, somewhat somber and mean-looking man pokes his head in through the side window of the cab. He is a guard. He inquires, "What do you want?"

Myron responds, "We are Mr. and Mrs. Myron Bright, from Fargo, North Dakota, and we have an appointment with the president of the United States at 12:45 p.m. "

"What do you got for identification?" Myron digs around in his wallet and finds an identification card. It's an Elks membership card for the lodge in Fargo.

The officer is satisfied and the cab is allowed to proceed to the southwest side of the White House.

The couple leaves the cab and they enter a small hallway on the ground level. Another officer stops them and asks for identification. This time Myron pulls out a different card. It's bronze in color and designates that Myron Bright is a member of the Democratic-NPL (for Nonpartisan League) Party of North Dakota.

This card satisfies the officer. After checking the Bright name on the visitors register, he escorts the couple into the room on the lower level of the White House.

Fritzie and Myron wear a slight smile and they relax and smoke a cigarette for a few moments.

A man appears and says, "Hello, come with me."

They do.

The three crowd into a rather tiny elevator, get a lift up to the first floor on the west wing of the building and are taken to a large, brightly lit, elegantly furnished room called the Fish Room.

This room, rectangular in shape, but with an oval wall at one end, carries a red and white motif in its furnishings. The room obviously had use as a conference and press room. A round table in the center could seat ten people. One end of the room contained a speaker's dais with microphones attached, all in front of a fireplace.

A framed letter signed by Thomas Jefferson is perched atop one of the desks. The letter in Jefferson's hand reports on his activities as ambassador to France. It refers to the construction of a Fahrenheit thermometer and also comments on botanical sciences.

Myron and Fritzie focus their eyes on the beautiful furnishings, the memorabilia going back to the beginnings of this country, and a lovely bouquet of spring flowers on the table in the center of the room. All is quiet at that moment.

Myron looks at Fritzie and Fritzie returns the gaze. The same thoughts come to both of them: "Only in America."

Here they were. Both first-generation Americans. Both Jews. Myron is the first lawyer of the Jewish faith ever nominated to serve as a federal appellate judge on the U.S. Court of Appeals for the Eighth Circuit, which encompasses a seven-state area consisting of Minnesota, the two Dakotas, Iowa, Nebraska, Missouri and Arkansas.

How did this come about?

Myron's mind, in the several minutes in the Fish Room, like a fast-frame movie, quickly reveals his almost fifty years of life. He tries to make sense of this important but unusual development, which would turn him, a trial and appellate lawyer with a taste for politics, into one of the about ninety-five active circuit judges in the United States.

His mind races backwards. He thinks about his twenty-one years as a lawyer in Fargo, his wins and losses, his important cases and those not so important but nevertheless meaningful. All of those matters rush through his momentarily closed eyes.

He thinks through his dozen years of political activity, a time that seems detached from reality. He realizes politics helped get him here and it comes to mind how it all started. Many years earlier, in 1954, he had run for Democratic precinct committeeman, in Fargo. Myron and his opponent — the latter representing a different faction of the Democratic Party — tied in the voting. Myron became the precinct committeeman by winning a coin flip.

As precinct committeeman, he became a very active worker in Democratic-NPL politics, moving up to party chairman of Cass County, the most heavily populated county in North Dakota.

Myron also thinks about his war service. His four years serving in the United States and overseas seem like another era, but those years contributed a great deal toward his willingness to be a judge.

In his mind, Myron wonders whether it was luck, chance or maybe divine intervention. Perhaps all played a role in bringing him to this place on this date, May 8, 1968.

How lucky could I be, Myron thinks. I chose to be a lawyer instead of a businessman. If I had gone the other way, I would not be here. I became a lawyer and was presented the choice of practicing with a gentile law firm in Fargo rather than with a Jewish lawyer in Duluth, Minnesota. I chose Fargo. Was that luck or predestination?

Myron thinks about his relationship with Senator Burdick. It seemed that by accident, Myron was in Minot, North Dakota, trying a lawsuit in 1955 at the same time Quentin was in the Magic City (Minot). Myron's lawsuit was in federal court while Quentin was in state court. Quentin collapsed and his illness was brought to Myron's attention. Myron called Bill Bearman, a friend in Minot; Bearman called his doctor and the doctor came to see Quentin, gave him medication and arranged to send him back to Fargo. Myron helped make those arrangements. A casual friend until then, Burdick became a close friend of Myron's after these events.

Myron muses: Fritzie and Myron helped in a big way to make Quentin Burdick a congressman in 1958 and a senator in 1960. Now Quentin's recommendation to the president had made Myron a federal judge.

Myron's thoughts and reminiscences recall the political theme of meeting with and working with some of the country's most prestigious people and political leaders after World War II. They included: John Kennedy, first a U.S. senator and later president; Lyndon Baines Johnson, U.S. congressman, senator, vice president and later president; Kennedy's brother Robert, an attorney general and later a U.S. senator of New York; other members of the Kennedy family; and Orville Freeman, a law school classmate and governor of Minnesota, and secretary of agriculture in the Kennedy and Johnson administrations. Myron thinks about his state leaders, too, such as William Guy, a close friend and governor of North Dakota from 1961 through 1972, and many others in the political world from both parties.

Myron also thinks about his fortunate early life of obtaining a wonderful education in the grade school, junior and high schools and junior college of Eveleth, Minnesota. In addition, he remembers the melting pot communities of the Mesabi Iron Range, in northeastern Minnesota, communities inhabited by persons of different ethnic backgrounds. Almost everybody there had immigrated from eastern and central Europe and Russia, where, in spite of varying religious differences and ethnic backgrounds, all of the young people got along beautifully. Almost all were first-generation Americans, like Myron. People there were judged by their individual merit and not their race or religion. Tolerance, not prejudice, served as the watchword for those people living in the Iron Range communities.

Myron also remembers his father, Morris, a Russian immigrant, now deceased, who had worked long hours in his mercantile business to make it possible for the Bright children to have a college education. He thinks about his mother, Lena Bright, a loving person, and a talented and friendly and generous individual who recognized that her children must and should become educated. She took in boarders and roomers to help pay for the education of her children.

Myron also thinks about the Great Depression of 1929-1941 and up to the U.S. entry into World War II and his tough life in those days and, yes, how Myron's parents had worked hard and persevered and made a decent, middle class living.

Those memories are interrupted.

The door opens and in walks a tall, handsome, dark-haired young man in his late twenties. He greets the Brights with a warm hello and a handshake with the future judge.

"I'm Larry Temple, President Johnson's White House lawyer. I've seen the data on your background, Mr. Bright."

He continues, "I'm a graduate from the University of Texas College of Law. I congratulate you on your appointment. By the way, I think you should know that your appointment was made in the White House, not in the Department of Justice."

Myron would learn the whole story later.

Temple leaves the Fish Room. A few moments later, Burdick enters. The three exchanged greetings when the door opens again. In walks a young man wearing a pair of prominent horn-rimmed glasses. He is a short Texan, about five feet seven inches.

"Hello, I'm James Jones, the president's appointment secretary."

Jones exchanges comments about the proposed visit with the president. He then escorts the Brights and Senator Burdick to the anteroom just off the president's office, the famous Oval Room.

The White House photographer enters. This gentleman of Japanese ancestry carries three cameras and keeps clicking the shutters as we talk.

Jones says, "The president will see you as soon as he finishes his telephone call." Jones then leads the three into a small hallway next to the Oval Room.

Myron could see just part of the Oval Office. He notes a secretary standing in front of the president's desk. These were the days of the miniskirts. Myron observes the secretary is wearing a very mini miniskirt.

After a moment, Jones pokes his head into the Oval Room.

He turns. "The president will see you now."

We enter the Oval Office. Our lives would never be the same.

I am the Myron Bright described in this introduction.

This book is a story of my life, the almost fifty years before I met President Johnson and forty-plus years thereafter. I am the longest-serving, working judge in the history of the Eighth Circuit Court of Appeals.

The story relates my background, both historically and as I see it now. It provides the background of how I became a federal judge and served more than forty-five years.

My years in North Dakota and national politics from 1956 until 1968 are important to this story. I believe this involvement has historical significance and should be of interest to all who remember that time personally or through reading. The era of Dwight Eisenhower, JFK, LBJ, Hubert Humphrey and Robert Kennedy represent exciting years — yes, a wonderful period in American history.

Finally, I have served as a federal judge during changing times.

In 1968, racism and discrimination against minorities and women served as the norm of our society. Much has changed. I was part of making that change.

How and why as a federal judge did I write and rule as I did during the civil rights revolution of my active years as a judge, 1968-1985?

What role have I played as a senior judge, since 1985?

Over that period, except for the eight Clinton years of 1992-2000, Republican presidents have generally appointed circuit judges who have far different backgrounds, as well as different judicial philosophies than mine, and the majority of the circuit judges who were colleagues from 1968 until 1985.

Myron H. Bright

In a sense, I take the words of a song sung often by the late Frank Sinatra: "You made me what I am today, I hope you're satisfied."

Here's the Myron Bright story — my story.

Goodbye Mike, Hello Judge: My Journey for Justice

SECTION ONE

— CHAPTER 1 —
The Bright Family

Family influences help in making us what we become in later years. Neither my father (Morris) nor my mother (Lena) talked much about the old days. As best as I can, here is what I learned about my parents.

Morris came from Jewish parents, fierce-looking people from their photographs, whom I never met and who never came to America. He once told me his family lived close to the Black Sea and were either fishermen or sold fish. He lived in Kagarlyk in The Ukraine (from immigration papers). That city or place seems unknown in today's world; I have not found the name on any old maps.

Morris had an older brother, Nochim (Sam), and one sister, Hinda (Ann). Hinda, with her husband, immigrated to this country in 1913, living in Philadelphia, when she was twenty-nine. That tells me she was the youngest child and the only daughter. One of my distant cousins told me he had heard there may have been another sibling, a boy, who did not like America and returned to his home country.

Morris's family remaining in the Ukraine perished in Russia, possibly in 1919 or later, when the Jewish settlements in that country experienced pogroms, a killing of Jews by the Ukrainians and Russians.

As best as I can piece it together, what follows is the story of the emigration. First, Nochim, the oldest brother, was drafted into the Russian army. As Morris told it, once you got into the Russian army, it was forever or until death. As a young man, Nochim's service took him near the Russian-German border. He deserted and somehow made his way across Europe. When he got to Liverpool, England, he contacted a Jewish agency that assisted him in getting passage, steerage class, I'm sure, to America—land of opportunity and of the free.

That is when a name change occurred. The story, as I remember it, describes an encounter between Nochim and the immigration inspector. The inspector could not pronounce the name that Nochim spoke, so the inspector decided he would give Nochim (our uncle) a better name. He said, "You look like a bright young man, so that is your name, Sam Bright."

That is how the Bright name came about. I am told the family name was originally "Kleinetsky," which in Yiddish could mean "clean." Morris's story echoes that of Nochim. He, too, suffered the draft into the Russian army when he reached age eighteen. He became a musical drummer. I can understand that background, for in later years, he frequently thumped to the music that was playing.

Again, his service brought him near the Russian-German border, where he deserted. Somehow he traveled across Germany and got to Liverpool. From Liverpool, he sailed to Quebec on a ship whose name he did not remember, traveled by train to Sault Ste. Marie, Michigan, and somehow arrived at the head of the Great Lakes—the harbor of Duluth-Superior.

In his declaration of intention to become a citizen, dated February 25, 1918, Morris described himself as a person of short stature, five-feet three and a half inches, weighing one hundred thirty-seven pounds. He stated he previously had lived in Kohorlik[1], Russia, where he had been born on January 27, 1882. He stated that he entered the United States at the port of Sault Ste. Marie via the Canadian Pacific Railway on July 24, 1905. At that time, he was twenty-three. He added in his declaration: "I am not an anarchist. I am not a polygamist, nor a believer in the practice of polygamy; and it is my intention in good faith to become a citizen of the United States so help me God."

Morris worked in the shipyards in Duluth and later became some sort of peddler.

I remember with affection and delight two consistent actions of Morris. One, the old-fashioned way he poured his tea into a saucer and then sucked the tea through a lump of sugar held in his lower lip. That is the way to drink tea.

Second, in an old-country tradition, he kissed his sons and daughter on the lips on their leaving from home or returning home. What a nice tradition!

Morris worked hard all his life. More about this later.

Lena gave me my life. As she told me many times, I needed a blood transfusion at birth. Lena furnished the blood, but complications ensued in the carrying of blood from mother to child and, as a result, all of the capillaries broke down in Lena's arm (the left one, as I recall) and left her with tissue paper-thin skin that would bleed on the slightest impact. Her arm color was a deep red, slightly lighter than the red blood below the skin. In order to cover this infirmity, she almost always wore long sleeves.

Lena was a real survivor. She was a warm, caring mother, a great worker, a baker of the highest order and a wonderful homemaker. When you tasted her bread or rolls (yum, yum!), there was none better.

While Lena never talked much about the old country, the following is as much of the story as I can put together. We do not have access to any immigration papers.

Lena's family came from Serint in Lithuania, then part of Russia. Lena always spoke of the old home as Vilna gebornon (born near or in Vilna) in what is now Lithuania, but in the 1800s it was part of Russia under the rule of the czar.

Lena's date of birth is in some dispute. Morris's petition for naturalization states his wife, Lena, as being born June 17, 1883, one year after Morris. However, it was a not-well-kept secret that Morris was younger than Lena by two or more years. Lena died on August 29, 1977. We thought she was ninety-nine; if so, her birth date would be 1878. Assuming that she was two years older than Morris, she would have been born in 1880 and was ninety-seven when she died. I was born on March 5, 1919. My birth certificate shows Morris was thirty-seven and Lena was thirty-eight, which would give her a birth date of 1881. Thus, Lena would have been ninety-six when she died in 1977. That is as close as I can do on the age business. She lived a good, long life and was keen mentally until the end.

Lena's maiden name was Levine. She was the oldest of four sisters. Her parents were Abe and Esther (Gutel) Levine. Abe and Esther were farmers in Lithuania, to the best of my knowledge. Lena and her father came to America in 1900, to Duluth. Lena worked in a factory as a seamstress and earned enough money to send for her sister Dora in 1901. By 1902, the rest of the family immigrated to Duluth, Lena's mother and her sisters, Rose and baby Sophie.

My parents married on December 30, 1906, in Duluth, and then moved to the small mining town of McKinley, part of the Mesabi Iron Range in northern Minnesota, as the iron ore mines in that range began opening. They operated a general store. The family came along soon: Joseph, the eldest, born February 7, 1908, in Duluth; Mabel Rose, born June 17, 1910, in Duluth; Leo, born February 13, 1913, in McKinley; Roy, born on January 25, 1915, in McKinley; and Myron, born on March 5, 1919, in Eveleth, although by this time Morris and Lena had moved their business about five miles west to Gilbert.

One might notice that Mabel and Lena have the same birthdays on June 17. Lena told me she did not know her birth date on the English calendar, so she took her birthday as the same day and month of Mabel's birth.

My parents did not live an easy life in McKinley. Lena spoke about carrying fresh water six blocks from a nearby pond or lake to provide for the family. Morris worked in the general store from morning to late at night. The store supplied both groceries and clothing. They made a good life for themselves and their children.

The general store in McKinley burned down, but I do not know whether it was before or after the move to Gilbert.

I have memories of the store in Gilbert and our life there. We lived on the main floor of the two-story house belonging to Morris. The house had running water and Lena cooked on a wood-burning kitchen stove. In the winter, we heated the house with a silver and black stove that had glass in the door. I remember the warm glow of the coals through the glass. In cold weather, and it really got freezing cold in northern Minnesota, you could be warm in the front but chilled in the rear when trying to keep warm staying close to that stove.

We had a six-room house with all rooms connected in a circular fashion — kitchen, dining room, living room and three bedrooms: one for my folks, one for my sister, Mabel, and one for the four boys. We slept two in a bed. I shared my bed with big brother Joe. Even though I was just a little boy in Gilbert, three events stand out.

The first occurred in the summer of 1921 or 1922. Morris owned a touring car called a Pan, manufactured in Minnesota. He also had stock in the corporation that owned the motor company. Morris lost it all when the

Pan (Pandolpho Company) went broke.

We lived on an inclined street (Minnesota Avenue) in Gilbert. Morris parked the Pan facing down the hill with the right front wheel against the curb. One day, Morris didn't set the brake. I got in the automobile to play my usual game of drive the car. I turned the wheel and the car rolled down the hill, through a wire fence and across the street into the yard of our neighbor, Tillie Rubenstein. At that time, one of the crowd that had gathered said, "Look at that Myron Bright. Only two and a half years old and already he's driving a car by himself." The moral of this tale is: Do not drive without driver's education.

The second in 1925 or 1926: My folks went to Chicago to visit Uncle Nochim and family. When they returned, they bought me a tricycle. How I loved to ride it! But Morris sent it back after I used it for a day or two. I never again rode a tricycle, and I did not own a bicycle until age fourteen, when I won a bike.[2] Morris said I was too old for the tricycle. I think the real reason was that he just could not afford that luxury.

The third, on my seventh birthday when I had received a new ball and bat from my parents: My big brother Roy (four years my elder) said to me as I was playing ball, throwing it in the air and catching it, "Let me hit the ball in the yard." I agreed and stood behind him. As he swung the bat back, it collided with my forehead and opened a large gash. Lena rushed me to the doctor, but she was afraid to authorize stitches. The doctor (Dr. Barrett) taped the broken skin together. I recovered, but I still carry a noticeable scar. The moral I learned is stay well behind the batter. I put that experience to use in my years as a catcher in softball games.

Roy served as both my hero and my nemesis. Once he offered me a ride on a bladed grass cutter. I accepted. Roy cut a big gash in my rear end. Fortunately, I could push the broken skin back in place without further harm.

I had reached the age of eight when the family moved in 1927 to Eveleth. My memories of wonderful days growing up there remain vivid.

Let me say a word about Eveleth, one of the mining towns on the Mesabi Iron Range. The Range generally extended from the cities of Biwabik and Aurora on the east in a wavering general east to west direction to Grand Rapids at the west end. Several cities grew up during the late 1800s into the early 1900s as industry began opening and developing mines for the high grade iron ore which ran in a band or range of approximately sixty miles. Most of the many communities were about five miles apart. I mentioned McKinley on the west, where my parents and family began their life in about 1906. The next town was Gilbert, about five miles to the west, population about 2,500. Next, another five miles west to Eveleth, where my family moved in 1927 after Gilbert.

I consider Eveleth my home town. The name of Eveleth came from a timber cruiser named Erwin Eveleth.

Nicknamed the hilltop city, Eveleth boasted a population of nearly eight thousand in 1927 and indeed was built on a hill, where the schools were located, and then sloped several hundred feet to the location of a large open pit mine on the lower reaches of the city.

Morris and Lena operated a department store in Eveleth named the Fair Store. In the Eveleth Centennial newspaper of July 3, 1992, the following flashback appears under the "Remember" column: "The Fair Store with everything in it from shoes, three piece men's suits to suitcase — a veritable department store. Mr. Bright was eager to bargain and sell."

I worked in the store from my early days, selling and cleaning up. I liked selling, but hated being on my feet. I had no ambition to be a merchant.

I mention the melting pot aspect of Eveleth. Immigrants came from central and eastern Europe primarily to work in the mines. The principal ethnic groups were Serbs and Slovenians from the then-Yugoslavia area of central Europe, Italians, Finns, a few Scandinavians, a few Cousin Jacks (Welsh miners), a few Jews, and a smattering of other nationalities. Oh, yes, we also had a few Greeks, French, and Chinese and a number of Irish. The names are of interest. I know of no African Americans or Hispanics. I'll list a few names of classmates to provide a picture of their diversity.

At random, here are a few of my classmates and friends:
    Marie Ciagne — Italian
    Donald Jarvey — Finnish
    Maxine Larson — Scandinavian
    Angeline Mattei — French
    Robert Orchard — Cousin Jack
    Frank Tassoni — Italian
    June Tregenza — Slovenian
    Frank Udovich — Slovenian

At the Fair Store, Morris employed as salespersons all women, one who spoke Slovenian, one who spoke Italian and one who spoke Finnish. Many of the immigrant parents did not speak English fluently.

Speaking of nationalities, *Ripley's Believe It or Not* articles noted that Eveleth had an "ichy" high school basketball team. Every player's name ended in "ich," i.e., Miroslavich, Lenich, Babich, etc. The predominant nationality was Slovenian and Serbians; next was Italians, followed by the Finns.

I learned early to understand and appreciate the diversity of my friends and their parents. We were all in the same boat to sink or swim, and swim we did.

I was the only Jewish person in my class and one of only a few in the entire student body. At the age of eight, I thought that I was the toughest guy around. I soon learned that I was not. I got knocked around in a fight with one John Riccelli, an Italian boy. I knocked him around, too. After that experience, I decided peace was better than a good fight. However, that fight reminded me anti-Semitism existed because our tussle started when John made some derogatory remarks about the Jewish religion.

Even though many parts of the country were rife with racial antagonisms against Jews, a story told in the movie *Gentlemen's Agreement*, there was little, if any, of that in Eveleth. However, with the activities of the Ku Klux Klan and the Nazis in Germany and America, I became well aware of anti-Semitism in America.

Regular religious services were held for about twenty families in the Eveleth Synagogue. Most of the breadwinners were retail merchants. While we had no rabbi in the city, we did have a learned man, Mr. Cohen, who taught us to read Hebrew well enough to qualify for a Bar Mitzvah ceremony through which a Jewish boy at age thirteen becomes a man for religious purposes.

Diversity was respected in the community. While there were relatively few Jewish students in the public schools, many of the Jewish students were leaders in scholarship, extracurricular endeavors and athletics.

Academics and sports were important in the Iron Range cities. Because of the taxes paid by the companies owning and operating the mines, the community and its schools were well funded. We had great public schools in Eveleth extending from kindergarten through high school and into a two-year junior college.

In all, that added up to fourteen years of free education, including books and supplies. I started third grade at Fayal School and completed through the sixth grade there. Almost all of my high school classmates continued in Eveleth Junior College. Most went on to graduate from other colleges and many to further education degrees.

I developed a wide base for my girlfriends. Audrey was probably German, but I never asked; Bunny, English, I think; Marie, Italian; Frances, I don't know, but she was beautiful and a talented actress type; Helen Bayuk, probably Slovenian, but I never asked; Helen Juntilla, Finnish. And there were many more.

As my senior resume of activities discloses, I was in almost everything except music. The high school yearbook summarized my activities, Hi-Y, president, 3, 4; class president 3, 4; class play; N. F. L., vice-president, 4; debate, 2, 3; dramatics, thespians; open pit, assistant editor, 3; *Carbide* editor; football, 3, 4; basketball, 3; intramural sports; Quill and Scroll, president 4; National Athletic Scholarship Society. I lettered in football two years, played basketball but did not letter.

At graduation, the American Legion awarded me the American Legion Medal for being the outstanding male graduate in athletics and scholarship.

Junior college was a continuation of high school but with many new friends who came from surrounding communities. I played football for two seasons. We were conference champions in 1938. I also debated, including in a National Junior College tournament; acted; served as freshman class president; partied and dated a lot; and received a great two additional years of education.

But all was not peaches and cream. My parents were observant Jews. To them, it would be a great sin for a Jewish boy to marry a non-Jew — a shicksa (gentile), as Lena would say. But it was bound to happen in the sort of society we lived. My brothers and I dated non-Jewish girls for the most part. There were few of our religion from which to pick.

When my oldest brother, Joseph, fell in love and married a beautiful blonde, Catholic lady from Virginia, Minnesota, named Rochelle George, all hell broke loose. Lena threw Joe's clothes out of the house. Lena and Morris sat shiva, which is a Jewish memorial practice to agonize over the death of a loved one. To them, Joe had died.

Lena, in an irrational state, blamed Uncle Henry Lippman for the debacle about Joe and insisted that Morris get his brother-in-law Henry Lippman out of the Fair Store in Eveleth. Henry had married Lena's younger sister Rose and was a partner in the store.

This was a hardship for the entire Lippman family, my cousins Milton (Mickey), Eleanor and Myron, and my Aunt Rose and Uncle Henry Lippman. Lena said something like, "If Joe could have worked in the store business, he would not have married a shicksa." The thinking was not true in my judgment but disclosed the agony of old-country Jewish parents who could not abide intermarriage.

Did it affect my seeing gentile girlfriends? No. But when I did, Lena admonished, "Don't marry a shicksa."

I'm sure that experience of the family played a role in my eventually marrying within the faith some years later. But it made no difference to brother Roy, who married Rochelle, a beautiful girl of Scotch descent during the World War II years. Those were the family travails. The pain eased somewhat when Leo married a nice Jewish girl in 1937, Billie Jean, and my sister, Mabel, stayed within the faith by marrying a Jewish boy in 1933, Harry Manfield of Sterling, Illinois.

My folks eventually accepted Rochelle into the family. Of all the in-laws, she cared for and helped Lena and Morris in their older years.

Let me digress to discuss my parents and my siblings in Gilbert and Eveleth.

The oldest of the Bright children, Joseph, and the second child and only girl, Mabel, graduated from Gilbert High School. Both were great students and prominent in school activities. Joe matriculated at the University of Minnesota and became a fine lawyer. He practiced for a time in Eveleth and later became an assistant attorney general for the state of Minnesota. At the end of Joe's career, he served as the Reviser of Minnesota Statutes. In school, Joe was a leader in academics, debated and played the violin. Joe, after retirement, served on the Minnesota State Employee Retirement Fund, and under his leadership, the fund increased pensions each year.

His activities as a lone scout led to a family nickname of "Hucka," which later applied to the remaining Bright boys — Leo, Roy and Myron.

This is the story: Joe's lone scout group met in a barn behind our home when we lived in Gilbert. The password to enter came from the American Indian language and sounded like the word "huck" or "hucka." The young scouts referred to the place as the "hucka" barn. Soon they applied the appellation to Joe, whom they called Hucka. The name did not stick to Joe, but later applied to Leo (Big Hucka), Roy (Middle Hucka) and Myron (Little Hucka). Roy and I both carried the nickname Hucka while we lived in Eveleth. Whenever I go back for a visit to Eveleth, my old friends still call me Hucka.

Turning to Mabel: She was a beautiful, generous person, played piano very well, went to teachers' college in Superior and taught school in Wisconsin until her marriage.

Lena insisted that her children receive a college education. To make it possible in the earlier days in Eveleth and Gilbert, she took in meal boarders and rented a room in our house to a local teacher. The receipts went to educate Joe and Mabel.

Now for my college years away from home.

— CHAPTER 2 —

Law School Daze

Nearing graduation from Eveleth Junior College in the spring of 1939, I faced the same nagging problem of many young adults — selecting a probable vocation and deciding where to pursue the necessary education. My interests at that time were in advertising and the law.

I had more than a passing interest in becoming a lawyer. My oldest brother, Joseph, had practiced law in Eveleth for a short time before taking a position as an assistant attorney general with the state of Minnesota. I spent many an hour reading short excerpts of law cases at his Eveleth office, and I found them to be of great interest. And, since I had been a very good debater in high school and in junior college, I considered studying law as well.

However, the United States, and the Iron Range in particular, were suffering mightily from the Great Depression, which began with the stock market crash in 1929 and continued into the 1940s. Jobs were scarce as were opportunities for lawyers. Brother Joe, a very able attorney, could not make a living practicing law in Eveleth. The profession simply did not look very promising for a young man as I learned that a law degree could very well be a route to starvation rather than success. I was not certain what vocation to follow.

To alleviate my growing uncertainty about my future life's work, I sought assistance from a counseling service at the University of Minnesota, which operated a testing bureau to determine student aptitude and likelihood of success in studying various college programs and vocations.

Upon completion of the tests in the summer of 1939, I talked with an advisor who indicated that I possessed a good aptitude for either the law or the advertising field. As I recall that conversation, the counselor edged me toward law school, and stated that I would have nothing to lose and could always switch my course of study after the first year. He added, "You won't hurt yourself by learning a little bit of law."

I took that sage advice and enrolled at the University of Minnesota Law School in the fall of 1939. The school offered a "two/four" course of instruction, which required a high school diploma, two years of undergraduate education and four years of law school. The school also offered an alternative for college graduates who could obtain a law degree after only three years of study. I qualified for the two/four year course of study.

Thank goodness I followed the advice of that counselor so many years ago, for I discovered a "brave new world" and developed a life-long love for the study of law. To me, reading and analyzing case law served as an inviting challenge, like solving an intricate puzzle. And this would serve me well in the days and years to come.

The freshman class of 1939 consisted of about 120 students (all male but one), many of whom had undergraduate degrees from prestigious institutions such as Harvard and Yale. Many had distinguished backgrounds such as Pierce Butler III, the grandson of a United States Supreme Court justice from St. Paul. Still others had graduated with four-year degrees from the University of Minnesota. Frankly, I was overawed. Here I was, just a small-town boy with a two-year degree from a minor junior college, in the midst of all those lofty degrees and high qualifications.

Yet, to my delight, these young men proved to be a group of friendly and collegial fellows. During the fall quarter, I lived in Pioneer Hall, a dormitory, where I studied hard, but also found time to make friends with the other law students who lived there. While we all strove for good grades, the competition was friendly and not cutthroat as happened to be the case in many major law schools. Often, after morning classes, we met for lunch and discussed the professors' lectures and the cases of the day. As we pondered, postulated and pontificated about the morning law sessions, I felt as though all my friends seemed to know a great deal more than I about the law.

In the law school classrooms, students were assigned seats in alphabetical order. The A's were down in front followed by the B's, C's, D's and so forth. Students with names at the far end of the alphabet sat in the backs of the classrooms. I sat with two wonderful B's. On my left was Irving Brand of Minneapolis. He later became a great lawyer and an excellent state judge in Minnesota. On my right sat David Brink, who became one of my best friends, later served as an attorney in a prestigious Minneapolis law firm, and still later in 1981-82 became president of the American Bar Association. David and I remain good friends.

The law school faculty, although small, consisted of very able and highly regarded law instructors. Of particular note were the following: Professor Everett Fraser, dean of the law school and professor of real property law; Professor William Prosser, who taught torts and bailments; and Professor Horace Reed, my contracts professor, who became a good friend. Prosser became a prominent authority in tort law, and later served as dean of the law school at the University of California in Berkley, where he established himself as an esteemed scholar.

In law school, all of the classes proceeded on the Socratic method. We were assigned various cases to read, analyze and present in class. All students had book-style bound notebooks in which to take notes. When assigned a particular case, a student would compile a short brief, noting the facts of the case together with the decision, as well as commentary on the legal reasoning. In class, the professor would ask a student to present the facts of the case and then proceed with inquiry and discussion, asking for participation from any and all students. It was with fear and trepidation that I answered a professor's question, and therefore tried to stay out of the limelight as much as possible. Often after class a number of students would gather around the professor to ask questions and seek further information. As a first-year law student, I felt I did not know enough to be part of those gatherings.

During my first quarter of law school, I put in long, hard hours of study, often reading my assigned materials until the early morning hours like 2:00 a.m. Unfortunately, my scrupulous attention to my studies had an adverse effect in the classroom. Classes generally started at 8:00 a.m. Sometimes I would doze off during one or more of these early sessions; when I did, my note-taking via pen and ink would dribble off the page. Often I had to ask one of my friends to complete my notes. This routine of late studying and nodding off during the lecture periods became a vicious cycle, and one that I did not break until the second year.

Although I thought that most of my classmates knew far more law than I and performed much better in the classroom, I was proven wrong when we were subjected to our first law school test in late December. This first test, which was a practice exam (all essay), demonstrated that I was doing all right. To my amazement, I ranked sixth in the class. The other B's, David Brink and Irving Brand, did well also. Another friend, Orville Freeman (future Minnesota governor and later U.S. secretary of agriculture) came in eighth. Top of the class honors, however, went to two other good friends, Sam Berman and William Mussman, who continued to lead the class in scholarship all through our law school years.

Full of pride at my high class ranking, I became a little careless about my studies the following quarter. When the practice exams came along, I expected to do much worse as I had fudged a bit on my daily study hours. However, to my amazement, my class rank had slipped by only two notches with, as I recall, Orville Freeman taking my place as sixth. My saving grace was a grade of 100 in the real property course. And, proud was I when the dean publicly acknowledged my achievement, and if memory serves, my classmate and friend Mussman wrote an examination that scored 100 as well.

With two successful practice examinations and some good grades to my credit, I thought I was finally on my way and did not need to worry too much about grades. Not true. I became a little more careless in my studies, played a little more tennis, and spent a little more time with the opposite sex. The end result of my "little more of this and a little more of that" was a slip in my grades.

The final examinations in June proved to be academically challenging for me, and for others as well. Half of the students who began as fledgling law students in September failed and would never return. I slipped to a rank of somewhere between twenty-fifth and thirty-fifth, and instead of having a B average, I had to suffer the indignity of a C+ average, which was not enough to get me what I wanted most at the time — to be on the editorial board of the *Minnesota Law Review*, the school's student legal publication. It was a hard lesson that served me well. I made up my mind to spurn overconfidence and pledge myself to a better course of study when I returned to school the following fall.

During my second year at the University of Minnesota School of Law (1940-1941), a number of outside events, both worldly and within my own little sphere, made concentration on studies much more difficult. First, there was the escalating war in Europe and the sobering realization that the world was in peril should Adolph Hitler, dictator and vicious anti-Semite that he was, win the war in Europe and conquer Great Britain. Second, there was the impending draft, and many of those students of law and learning would eventually lay their books down and take up arms.

But, in the fall of 1940, other interesting things and events occurred that were closer to my heart and mind, and eventually distracted me from my much needed studies — classical music, playing tennis and falling in love. I acquired my appreciation of classical music, oddly enough, in my fraternity.

As was the case with so many students, comfortable housing became a major concern. I was not particularly enamored of dormitory life, and private housing was difficult to locate on the campus at the University of Minnesota. To escape this dilemma, I joined a fraternity. Although there were many fraternities on campus, I chose a Jewish fraternity knowing that Jewish students would not be accepted in others. I understood the unwritten law and did not try to cross that barrier. Phi Epsilon Pi, one of the two Jewish fraternities on campus, became home to me, and it was there that I made some lasting friendships. One was Morrie Jaffee, another product of the Iron Range. Also, Howard Sachs from Iowa, who later became dean of the law school at the University of Connecticut. Jaffee and Sachs studied law to the tune of classical music. As the radio blared, I, too, acquired a love for that very special musical genre.

While in law school, Jaffee served as an usher for the then highly regarded Minneapolis Symphony Orchestra, which played at the huge Northrop Auditorium on campus. The orchestra was led by the great conductor Demitri Metropolis, who later became conductor of the world-renowned New York Symphony Orchestra. On occasion, I substituted for Jaffee as an usher and delighted in the sounds of those great symphony concerts. I can still remember my first such experience and the conductor leading the orchestra in a fabulous rendition of the "Star-Spangled Banner." It was wonderfully different from hearing the national anthem played by piano or small band. I can still recall the beauty of it and the tears of joy running down my cheek.

I also played a great deal of tennis. At the end of my first year, I had participated in a number of tennis tournaments among the university male students and was able to earn my University of Minnesota freshman numerals (high rank). Even though my class standing was a junior, in athletic competitions I was ranked as a freshman and could not compete in the varsity team. Nevertheless, I pursued the sport while my law books stood idle.

Then, to complicate matters, I fell in love with a wonderful young lady named Betty Silver. She was pretty, shapely and bright, and worked as a legal secretary. To my mother's delight, she was Jewish. I was twenty-two and she was eighteen, and although it was young love, we both believed it was true love. I saw a great deal of Betty Silver that spring quarter.

In addition to my extra-curricular activities, I contracted a severe case of the flu during the early winter months of 1941. It lasted for several weeks and I ended up in the university's hospital, where I was finally cured of this debilitating illness. Although I was able to attend most classes, my after-class studying was limited as I was too weak, tired and ill.

In spite of all these occurrences, both good and bad, my second year of law school proved to be better than the first. I managed to do quite well on the final examinations and raised my ranking by about ten places. However, I still achieved less than a B average — again not good enough to serve on the *Minnesota Law Review*.

Throughout the summer of 1941, world events would change forever the names and faces of my third-year class. Some failed to make acceptable grades; still many others left for military service in response to the national draft. Too, several of my classmates were reserve officers or volunteered for military duty in order to obtain a commissioned status. It was my intention to serve in the military as well, but I had been rated by the draft board for noncombatant service because of my nearsighted vision. So, for the present I would remain in school.

During my third year, the escalating war in Europe cast a long shadow and was ever-present in our minds. I had moved out of the fraternity house and took up residence in a private home with a fellow I had met named Lionel Greenberg. He was a first-year student in the law school and hailed from North Dakota. He and I became good friends and we got along quite well.

As America prepared to wage the "war to end all wars" in the spring of 1942, the remainder of my third year was filled with long study hours, but nonetheless, was an enjoyable time, both academically and socially. As the housing situation in the private dwelling declined, I along with three others, including Harold Ladin of Chisholm, Minnesota (another Iron Range town), found a suitable four-room apartment near campus. Determined to raise my class standing, I changed my study habits to work on my courses during reasonable hours, and I stayed awake during classes. By the end of the term, I had raised my grade point average to a B. Now, I was eligible to serve on the *Minnesota Law Review,* and I looked forward to a rewarding senior year. But this was not to be, for in July of 1942, I was drafted into military service. My romance with Betty did not survive the war years. She wanted to get married to me, but I did not want a war bride. We parted, and she married another.

— CHAPTER 3 —

Private to Sergeant to Commission

December 7, 1941, will be remembered as that date in infamy when the Japanese attacked this country by bombing Pearl Harbor. It also began a four-year interruption in my legal education.

That Sunday has become etched in my memory. I returned to my room in a private dwelling, when the lady of the house said, "You have a telephone call, Myron."

I answered the telephone. My brother Joseph's wife, Rochelle, gave me the news. She said, "Myron, don't expect to see your brother Roy for a long time. The Japanese have just bombed Pearl Harbor."

Four years my senior, Roy had entered the Army Air Forces several months earlier and on December 7 was serving in the Seventh Air Force, stationed at Hickam Field in Hawaii, which had just been included in the bombing run at Pearl Harbor.

Roy, later a highly decorated airman (seventeen decorations), fortunately had left Hawaii a few days earlier for the mainland with other airmen to pick up and deliver to Hickam Field a number of B-17 airplanes. Roy missed the Pearl Harbor catastrophe but flew into Honolulu a few days later.

I knew then I would be going into military service. I was subject to the military draft and it was only a matter of time until Uncle Sam would call.

However, I still needed to finish off my third year at the law school. A number of my classmates had already entered the service and more, almost all the class, would be in the military by the end of 1942.

In December 1941, I made a note in one of my law class bound notebooks predicting the war would end in four years. How right I was; the war concluded in August 1945, almost four years later.

The Bright boys served their country well. Joseph, the oldest and then in his thirties, served in the Army stateside. Roy saw active duty from early 1941 until the end of the war and continued in the Air Force Reserve for many years thereafter, retiring as a colonel. I entered service at Fort Snelling, Minnesota, on July 6, 1942, as a lowly private earning then twenty-one dollars per month, and terminated active military service as a captain May 28, 1946, about two months short of four years.

I recall a number of experiences as a soldier, not a mere chronological tale. I did my duty as best I could and qualified for war medals with two bronze stars, not for shooting of the enemy, but because I served overseas in two theatres of war — the India-Burma, Central Burma campaign, as part of the Asia Pacific War Campaign.

Let's start at the beginning. I lived in a tent at Fort Snelling for a few days. My then love, Betty Silver, came over crying and concerned. I believe I got some time off, but not much, for romance with her. Soon the military shipped me to Fort Leonard Wood in Missouri. There for six weeks, I trained to be a soldier.

I remember my experiences on the rifle range best of all. What a disaster! I had hunted with a gun only once when a school chum, Alvin Axelson, who lived on the outskirts of Eveleth, invited me to shoot rabbits with him. He furnished me a .22-caliber rifle. When a rabbit jumped out of the woods and sat about six feet away from me, I pointed the gun (but did not aim) at the rabbit and fired. I missed. The rabbit looked up at me, and if rabbits laugh, he or she laughed, and hopped happily into the woods.

That sort of foreshadowed my "success" on the rifle range. We fired away at targets about fifty yards away. After our shooting, soldiers in the trench behind the targets would put up a white circular marker to show where in the target bullet holes appeared. The object, of course, was for the shooter to hit the center, the bull's-eye of the target.

I never found the bull's-eye. Indeed, I never even hit the target, so I received notice of poor marksmanship by a red flag on a stick, which waved back and forth. The soldiers called that red flag "Maggie's drawers."

Later in my military career, I qualified as an expert sharpshooter or marksman with various firearms ranging from a machine gun to a pistol.

At basic training, I made many new friends from all over the country. We learned, marched and bitched about the Army and the low pay but developed a great camaraderie. A couple of my law school friends were in my training outfit. I also met and got to know Betty's brother, Abe Silver.

The six weeks passed quickly. One unforgettable incident should have been forgettable. Near the end of the six weeks of training, I received a pass to leave the fort. A couple buddies and I spent the next few hours in a local tavern drinking highballs. Yes, I became a bit drunk but somehow held myself up straight enough to pass the camp guards and enter the Fort. I went to my barracks (I thought) to turn in. To my chagrin, I discovered another body in my bed. I woke the soldier saying, "You're in my bed." Like hell! I was in the wrong barracks. Of course, they all look alike.

In September, my group of Quartermaster Corps trainees shipped out to the mountains of Colorado and Camp Hale, where the ski troops were in training.

Does luck play a part? Let me tell you the story about my first promotion.

During the first day or so at Camp Hale, I got assigned to "KP" (kitchen police) in the kitchen and mess hall, which requires very monotonous, hard work. We spent much of the time cleaning pots and pans and scrubbing the floors. But more than that, the sergeant in charge gave me the outside job of digging a ditch.

I busied myself at this back-breaking task when a savior appeared in the guise of a second lieutenant. I have no record of his name and will call him Arnold Block for the purpose of this story.

Block had looked over the qualifications of the new trainees and noted that I had a college degree as well as three years of law school. He said to me, "Private Bright, I am the purchasing and contracting officer of this military base. I want you as my first assistant, and I will make you a technical sergeant, the second-highest rank (then) for an enlisted man."

Glory be! I got out of that ditch in a split second, changed into a clean uniform and worked with him to set up and operate the purchasing and contracting office for the base.

After about two or three weeks, Block recommended me for a promotion to staff sergeant, but instead I was promoted to a regular sergeant, with three stripes on my sleeve, rather than four as a staff sergeant or five as a tech sergeant. As I recall, the older Army personnel objected to some of us newcomers receiving a quick promotion, so the commander of my outfit thought it best to go a bit slow.

Serving as a sergeant presiding over the Purchasing and Contracting Department was a warm and enriching experience. With this new position, I was free on weekends and generally traveled by bus from our base high in the mountains in the rarified air of about ten thousand feet, to Denver, about sixty miles to the east.

At Denver, I met up with old friends such as Bill Siegel, my tennis-playing doubles partner from Eveleth, and others from the Iron Range. We partied, drank and generally enjoyed life on the weekends. I even dated some.

I'm set for the war years, I thought to myself. I will be a purchasing and contracting officer, get promoted to tech sergeant and live a good life at Camp Hale. I envisioned a furlough for the coming December and entertained warm, romantic thoughts about seeing my love, Betty, again. I thought marriage to Betty could work out since I had a good position at Camp Hale.

The best laid plans often go awry. When I returned from a trip to Denver in late fall, all had changed. The P & C office now became manned, or should I say "woman-ed," by female personnel. Unbeknownst to me, the Army brass had decided to staff it with civilians to relieve us soldiers from this noncombatant service so we could go to war. I became unemployed as a P & C sergeant but did stay to train my civilian-woman replacement.

Seeing the writing on the wall that I, as a sergeant, would soon be sent overseas, I decided to apply for the Quartermaster Officers Training School at Camp Lee, Virginia. I appeared before a screening committee of two high-level Army officers, met the qualifications and found myself en route to Camp Lee in mid-January 1943. This was my first trip to the South and I was shocked to see, firsthand, segregation of blacks in Petersburg, a city near Camp Lee. Gone was my planned leave in December, as well as any thoughts of a wedding with Betty.

I entered Camp Lee on January 16, 1943, for three months of officer training. We were called ninety-day wonders. I underwent vigorous instruction, both academic and nonacademic, learning to be an officer, to be a strong leader and an efficient person. I passed.

One incident stands out. A few days before graduation, I received a message: "Report to the company commander." Believe me, I shook with fright in my Army boots. What now?

I walked into the company commander's office, saluted and saw standing beside him an old friend of mine from days past, now an officer. I immediately recognized the officer as Myron (Mike) Marks, who had married a former longtime girlfriend of mine, Rita Schibel of Virginia, Minnesota. Marks was an infantry second lieutenant assigned to train officer candidates at Camp Lee.

Marks and his wife, Rita, and I had a nice reunion. A few days later when I marched in the graduation parade, Mike greeted and congratulated me. Rita then pinned on my second lieutenant officer's bars. Rita and Mike became my lasting friends. After the war, they lived in Virginia, Minnesota, on the Iron Range.

Earning my military commission gave me great pride and pleasure, exceeded in my life only once, when I became a federal judge many years later. It was a greater thrill than receiving the American Legion medal at Eveleth High School or my diploma on graduation from the University of Minnesota.

— CHAPTER 4 —

Officer and a Gentleman in the USA And En Route to India

My service as an officer in the Quartermaster Corps attached to the Air Force extended about three years, from April 1943 to May 1946.

The Army posted me to Pendleton Airbase in Pendleton, Oregon, but gave me a delay en route so I might visit my parents. I traveled first from Camp Lee to Minneapolis to see Betty and to encounter a crisis in my life. When Betty greeted me with love and showered me with her warm kisses, I had a sense that she wanted to marry. She did not make that request directly, but the hints became quite pointed like: "Now, Mike, you can support a wife," and "I'd like to be with you as much as possible even if you serve the country."

I was not ready for marriage. I believed I would be sent overseas, and didn't want the responsibility of a wife. I told those sentiments to Betty, left matters open and headed for my home in Eveleth. We arranged to see each other the next weekend, en route to Pendleton.

After visiting my home, I returned to Minneapolis the following Saturday. Betty and I had a wonderful, romantic weekend. Just before boarding a train to take me to Oregon came the bad news. Betty said, "Myron, I know how you feel. I love you very much, but I am going to marry my doctor friend who has been courting me."

I cannot remember whether I felt devastated or relieved. I could have changed her mind, but didn't say anything more except goodbye. It was a sad parting. Betty had been my real true first love, and I would never forget our time together. A small part of my heart and memory still holds some regret and warm thoughts of Betty. But after all these years, I know my life would have taken a much different turn had I said to her, "Let's get married."

I arrived in Pendleton, Oregon, in early May of 1943 to begin my service as an Army officer. I trained mostly to be a truck company officer. I learned much about following the chain of command and about the operations of a QMC (Quartermasters Corps) truck company. I even drove a "six-by-six" truck, as the Army vehicles were called. Shifting gears required double clutching, pressing the clutch down twice.

I enjoyed the city of Pendleton. Merchants and townspeople welcomed service personnel. I was a long way from home, but people there and everywhere in this country opened their homes, hearts and friendships to us in the military. I found a wonderful woman friend, companion and a great dancer. Her name was Nonee Smelcer. Our short but beautiful romance ended when I left the Pendleton Airbase in about March of 1943.

In early December of 1943, a group of quartermaster officers left truck company training and joined a newly organized 1084th Quartermaster Supply Company. The unit's mission was to service Air Force units with the basics of life, food, fuel, clothing, bedding and household-type supplies. The new commanding officer, C.E. Gallagher, appointed me supply officer for clothing, beds, tents, toilet paper (very important), blankets, pillows, sheets and whatever else was needed. The organization became part of the 61st Air Service Group, which consisted of several companies organized to service Air Force flying groups.

My military service required extensive training. I attended several classes to learn about quartermaster supply work and serving as an officer. In addition, I learned malaria control; did gas chamber exercises; learned about camouflage, automobile operations and maintenance; and completed an advanced course in quartermaster supply at Camp Lee in June and July of 1944. My company had been training at Fresno, California, during the early spring of 1944, and then moved to Lakeland, Florida, to prepare for overseas duty.

My education at the ordinance school at Fort Crook, Nebraska, (just outside Omaha) included the basics of engine mechanics and Army tank operation. I also met a very pretty young Jewish woman, Harriet Newman, with whom I had a rather interesting and serious dating relationship.

One rather humorous incident stands out. After driving a tank during the day, I drove the Newman family car on a date with Harriet that evening. I offered to drive the vehicle into the garage in the alley behind the Newman home. Harriet warned me that putting the car into the garage required careful maneuvering because the alley fronting the garage door was narrow. I said to Harriet, "Don't worry; I've just been driving a tank." I rammed the car directly into the garage, banging and damaging the car's front right fender on the garage door. So much for tank driving making me good behind the wheel of an automobile.

Granted a leave during this period, I invited Harriet to come to Eveleth and meet my parents. Unlike today's world and mores, we slept in separate rooms while there. My parents were so happy to see me dating a nice Jewish girl, they offered me the money to buy Harriet an engagement ring. I said no, I want to wait until after the war.

When I left Fort Crook and Omaha a few days later, Harriet gave me a lovely photograph that I treasured and took with me overseas. I think we understood she would wait for me until the end of the war and we probably would get married. It did not happen. (Instead I received a "Dear John" letter a year later when I was overseas.[3])

After Fort Crook, I returned to my unit, then training at an air base near Fresno, California. I have little recollection of those days except for memories about having some great times visiting in nearby San Francisco and also seeing my brother Joseph and his wife, Rochelle, in Stockton, California, close to his Amy base.

Later, in June of '44, I attended the advanced course for quartermaster supply officers at Camp Lee. For the first time, I lived with and worked with African American quartermaster officers. For me, it was an interesting and good experience, and those officers were certainly equal in ability to any of us.

On completion of this advanced course, I rejoined the 1084th, which had moved with the 61st Air Service Group to Lakeland, Florida, to prepare ourselves for overseas service. On August 29, 1944, at a ceremony on the Lakeland airbase, I received my promotion to first lieutenant. Several incidents occurred while we trained in Florida that may have had a long-running effect on my views, thoughts and perhaps my general philosophy of life.

It was at Lakeland that I first participated in military justice. The commanding officer, Colonel Cordero, appointed me defense counsel for a special court martial (military court of limited jurisdiction such as misdemeanor types of crimes) of one of the enlisted men in the group. The charge: Misconduct by urinating in a public place. Big deal!

The defense looked bleak. Military police caught him in the act. Ah, but I found a defense. It developed that the public place in fact was a private alley. My defense demonstrated that sometimes the obvious guilt is not so obvious and such a charge can be defended successfully on some occasions. Case dismissed.

The other experience off the military base occurred when we took a trip to a fancy resort near the ocean. At the registration desk, a sign read, "No Jews, Niggers, or Dogs allowed." I couldn't believe that such blatant discrimination on the basis of race, color or blood (dog or not) existed in this great country. I really thought about committing the military crime of urinating in that place but restrained my impulse.

Other experiences in Florida were great, such as ocean fishing, which I found to my liking.

After packing all of our military equipment, including guns rubbed with a lubricant called Cosmoline, the troops embarked for the long train ride west to a destination unknown. As events unfolded, I wished I knew where we were headed.

On the second day of travel, the train stopped at a location in Oklahoma near Fort Sill. The train commander, a major whose name I have forgotten, announced a two-hour layover. I and one enlisted man were assigned the pleasure of buying candy, cookies, cigarettes or anything else that the soldiers wished to have. We took orders and money and departed the station for two hours. We first headed for the nearest bar in the town to quaff a cold beer. As I write, I can almost recollect the cooling taste of that beverage.

With plenty of time, we leisurely accomplished our purchasing mission. Loaded with bags of sweets and other goodies, we returned to the railroad station and to our dismay we saw the rear end of the moving train, about a block away traveling west. Here we were — we did not know where the train was going. What a dilemma. I contacted the station master, but he was of no help. He did not know the troop train's destination either. What to do?

I called the officer of the day at Fort Sill. No help. Fort Sill operated as a cavalry post. A horse would do us no good. Finally, and in desperation, candy, the enlisted man and Lieutenant Bright boarded the next train going west. Visions of being AWOL crossed my mind, and I speculated about being in big trouble, maybe even considered a deserter.

We traveled on the civilian train for a few hours and around supper time arrived at another train stop. We got off, and to our pleasure, amazement and joy, we had caught up to our troop train, which was standing on another train track. Off we ran to the troop train. The GIs, with heads out of the open window, howled with laughter on seeing us.

We distributed the goods. The train commander said nothing to me. I had been spared from personal trouble. Lucky!

I found out our destination. We arrived at the Port of Los Angeles on September 25, 1944, and promptly embarked on the troop ship with hundreds of other military personnel. The vessel carried about six thousand passengers, enlisted men and a contingent of WACs (Women's Army Corps).

The women's quarters were, of course, in a separate section of the ship. The enlisted men were assigned to narrow bunks in the hold just wide enough for one person to sleep and piled eight high. The holds were crowded, somewhat smelly quarters. The enlisted men and women were served only two meals a day. It was the same for the officers, except that those assigned to supervisory duties in the GIs' quarters got three meals per day. At least in the officers' mess, where I ate, the cuisine was excellent.

Rather than the hold at the bottom of the ship, officers qualified for staterooms. I shared one with seven other officers. We slept in double-decker bunks.

On the evening of September 25, the ship's engine started up. At that time, I was serving in the hold as a supervisor for the GIs. I really thought we had begun our voyage and so did several GIs, who immediately became seasick. The next morning, I went on deck and discovered we had not left port. It was a rocky boat trip in the mind only.

We departed September 26, 1944, and sailed west without any escort. The ship zigzagged as a safeguard against a torpedo attack from a Japanese submarine. I believe we carried only one small cannon for protection.

After more than twenty days at sea, we finally tied up at the Port of Melbourne, Australia, where I again encountered military justice. The troops, officers and GIs left the boat and organized for a march on the dock. We paraded up and down for a short while and then returned to the ship. The commander ordered that all soldiers remain on board; we were not permitted to visit in Australia. The boat remained at dock for refueling overnight. A few enterprising GIs climbed off the ship in some way and visited this new country. Each of them, perhaps ten, were arrested and thrown in the ship's jail (brig) on their return.

The time came for charges and trial against the GIs who had unlawfully visited Australia. The commanding officer appointed me to defend them. The prosecutor, called advocate, was an officer named Perlman. I remember the name because of his conduct.

We made a deal. I would plead the first defendant guilty and Perlman would recommend to the judge (judge advocate) that the GI would be reprimanded but not serve any time in the ship's brig.

Perlman reneged. His word was not worth a wooden nickel. He recommended jail time for the duration of the voyage and the judge imposed that sentence.

Perlman had a law degree. I still needed another year of law school, but I knew more law than Perlman. I fixed his clock, so to speak. At the trial of the second GI, I tied Perlman up in knots with objections. He failed to prove the essentials of the charge. No one saw the defendant leave the ship and the military policeman who had arrested the defendant GI remained in Melbourne. Perlman could not prove his case. Case dismissed! End of prosecution for this second defendant and dismissal of charges against all the rest.

Then and now I abhor lawyers whose word is not worth a wooden nickel. Unfortunately, there are Perlman types whose word as a lawyer is not worth the paper on which it may be printed. That incident reminds me about the facts and circumstances decades later in *United States v. Norris*.[4] In *Norris* the prosecutor made a deal with the defendant, who pled guilty. The prosecutor then reneged on his word.

We sailed off to our destination, India. Two English destroyers accompanied and protected us in the sea route from Melbourne to India. I can still hear the *whoose, whoose,* the eerie whistle of the war ships as they maneuvered at various sides, forward and back of the troop ship. After several more days at sea and on October 29, 1944, we arrived at our then-CBI (China, Burma, India) theatre of war, docking at the western port and great Indian city of Bombay (now Mumbai).

My early months in the CBI were full of travel. We traveled west by rail to central India. We stopped at a military base in the Bihar province in central India to regroup, reorganize and retrain.

Later at another base (Shamshernagar), we participated with the Army Air Corps in its mission of flying the "hump," the mountains between India and China, to deliver munitions, petroleum and other supplies to our Chinese ally, General Chiang Kai-shek, whose troops were fighting the Japanese that had occupied and conquered much of that large country. That phase of operations ended in about June of 1945, when the Chinese Nationalist Army suffered defeat and loss of airbases to the Japanese.

One soldier in our 1084th in QM Company carried the nickname "Pop," a sergeant who had been in the military for over twenty years and was about in his mid-fifties. Pop qualified for immediate retirement. The trip overseas in the cramped, smelly quarters of the troop ship was difficult at best for any soldier, but particularly hard on him. Pop's health failed in some degree, and he decided to retire.

Our company commander, Captain Gallagher, a pipe-smoking Irishman from Boston, called out the whole unit in dress formation for a warm farewell to Pop. The company, about 120 men strong, with officers Gallagher, First Lieutenants James Miller of Seattle, Harry Stock of La Grande, Washington, Myron Bright of Eveleth, Minnesota, and Second Lieutenant Francis Murray of Superior, Wisconsin, arrayed in front of the troops who stood at attention. Pop perched in front of the formation, one foot on the running board of the Army six-by-six truck. The truck would deliver Pop and his gear to the nearby military airport and he could return to his home in the United States.

The company commander called out "Present Arms!" Those with weapons presented arms; the others saluted Pop. On behalf of all of us, the commanding officer said, "We wish you a fond farewell and a safe trip home."

With that one foot on the truck, Pop responded, "I give you all the old Army farewell: Goodbye, good luck and f— you." And off he went into the blue yonder.

From our training area in the Bihar province in central India, quite near the jungle, I was directed with other officers to lead a cadre of enlisted men to open a new airbase at a place called Shamshernagar, a railway siding or station, in the province of Assam, about 250 miles northeast of Calcutta.

Upon arrival by air at the new station, we found only bare accommodations. A company of U.S. Army engineers, assisted by a nearby British garrison of troops, was preparing the new airfield. It became my function with a small group of enlisted men to obtain supplies and living equipment to house the 61st Air Service Group. This unit, in turn, would service the Army Flying Group scheduled to arrive in a few months.

My first days at the new camp were challenging and interesting. We had flown to the new station in our 61st Air Service Group C4 7 cargo airship. Fortunately, I prevailed upon the pilot and senior officer of our group to furnish the plane to me and two of the enlisted men of my company.

The plane flew us to Calcutta, where the U.S. military had located supply warehouses. I was successful in obtaining a load of necessary supplies and equipment for the base. I also worked with the British military units and the engineers to beg or borrow what was needed to house the incoming troops.

I served at several airbases in India. My principal duties from about mid-November 1944 to June 1945 were as a quartermaster supply officer, later commanding officer of a truck company, and several other incidental duties.

Thereafter, I transferred to other airbase locations near Calcutta, where my unit began preparations for an invasion of Chinese territory. The dropping of the atomic bombs and the Japanese surrender in September 1945 changed all of that.

My task thereafter was to assist in disposing of Air Corps surplus, particularly old and junked airplanes. This included making arrangements to sell this scrap. One of my principal post-war duties was arranging for the sale of the scrap metal from wrecked military aircraft to Tata Steel Mills in Jamshedpur, India.

Although my unit participated in the Central Burma Campaign and the India-Burma Campaign as part of the Asia Pacific War Campaign, I did not shoot a gun at the enemy, nor did the enemy shoot at me. As is true in every war, there are those who fight the enemy and there are those behind the lines who provide support. I do not consider myself as a hero. I did the work assigned to me and gave these tasks my best effort.

I am proud that all through my military career, I received high ratings for my service. At the conclusion of my time with the 61st Air Service Group, commanding officer Colonel William Pocock Jr. wrote me a commendation letter. He noted that the strong reputation earned by our unit "is due, in a large measure, to the personal sacrifices made by you in the performance of your duties." He wanted me to know how much he appreciated my "loyalty and high spirit of cooperation."

In December, January and February, many of my officer and enlisted friends began their trips home in America. For about a month, January 19 to February 18, the military assigned me to stay at an officers' hotel in Calcutta. I had no duties, so I enjoyed a busy social life, made new friends and then finally departed India for the good old USA.

I have certain recollections of my extra service duties that bear on my later work as a lawyer and judge. These related to my legal services in the military while in India I cover in the next chapter.

— CHAPTER 5 —

Military Duties

Some of my military duties were reflective of my later life as a lawyer, law teacher and judge. In the early months at the Shamshernagar Airbase, October-December 1943, I received an appointment to serve as the advocate (prosecutor) in forthcoming special court martial cases. That appointment came from Colonel Cordero, a very able commanding officer. Cordero appointed his executive officer as the trial judge. I have forgotten his name but I will call him Lieutenant Colonel Alex Gardner. The defense attorney was a young lieutenant by the name of Robert Kunkel, who had no formal legal training.

Prior to hearing the first case assigned to us for trial, I ate breakfast with Gardner. He remarked about his new judge to be role stating, "We'll give him (any defendant) a trial and then I'll find him guilty."

My toast stuck in my throat. Military justice? Wow!

I reported the conversation to Kunkel to warn him of what was coming. Kunkel did what was needed. It took courage on his part. He promptly relayed the conversation to Cordero. I received a summons by way of a soldier assigned to the Group Headquarters to promptly report to Cordero's tent. His aide, Major Craft, brought me to the colonel's tent. I saluted and remained at attention, shaking in my shoes. I had no idea why I had been summoned and was standing ramrod straight before the commander. The interview lasted about one minute and can be capsulated as follows:

Cordero: Lieutenant Bright, did Lieutenant Colonel Gardner say to you that a court martial would try a soldier, and that Lieutenant Colonel

Gardner would find him guilty?

The commander fixed me with a steely-eyed glare. I could not lie even if I had a mind to.

Me: Yes, sir!

Cordero: Dismissed.

I saluted, did an about-face and left.

Gardner was relieved of duty and transferred out of the 61st Air Service Group by that evening.

A few weeks later, Cordero was replaced as commanding officer. The new commander returned me to my favorite position in the court martial scene — defense counsel.

A case developed that raised some interesting issues with unusual ramifications. Sometime in November or early December during a rainy monsoon season, a soldier in the Ordinance Company on night duty had left his headquarters post and taken a drive in his commanding officer's command car. The vehicle became stuck in a muddy road and the military police took the soldier into custody. His commanding officer, who I will call Captain LeRoy Pearson, proffered charges against the soldier, who I will call George McCabe, for using a military vehicle without permission.

As his counsel, I began my defense by interviewing the defendant. When we talked, McCabe looked me in the eye and gave this version:

> I was on duty at company headquarters. Around midnight, a young soldier came to my company's headquarters. The soldier said he was from the engineers outfit and that he got stuck while driving a truck that he was using to pick up heavy equipment. The guy asked me for help. I said sure and we took the command car and went to the place where the truck had become stuck. I helped him get the truck unstuck. After the solder left, I started back to my headquarters. The car got stuck. That is what happened.

Immediately a defense surfaced — implied consent to use the vehicle in an emergency.

I asked GI McCabe for the name of the soldier he had assisted. McCabe didn't know. To defend him, I needed that witness. So I did what any capable lawyer would do, put a notice up on the billboard at the engineers headquarters building.

What luck! In due time, a nice looking young GI with red hair and a great grin on his face showed up. I will call him Tom Morgan. He verified McCabe's version in every detail. We appeared for trial and the judge advocate was Major Francis A. Meagher. There may have been two other judges on the panel.

The prosecutor presented his case. Company Commander Pearson testified that McCabe, who was the duty soldier on the night in question, did not have permission to use the company's command car but was found with it at a place two miles from headquarters. In defense, McCabe gave his story.

Then I called Morgan. He was an impressive witness, telling the truth of what had occurred.

I argued that an emergency created an implied consent to use the command car. The verdict: Not guilty. What a great victory, I thought. Later, Meagher told me that Morgan had been a very persuasive witness. I figuratively patted myself on my back and went about doing my regular duties.

End of story?

Not quite. Come Christmas Eve day, 1944, I am a guest of the engineer company Christmas party for officers and GIs. Morgan came over to say hello. I remember his exact words spoken sixty-five years ago: "Lieutenant, we sure put one over on them."

I was shocked. "What, what are you saying?" I asked.

The response was something akin to the following: "Oh, you know it was a fake, a put-up job." He walked away.

What a dilemma for me. What should I do? I knew I should report the perjury. But then what? McCabe and Morgan would probably deny the perjury or else claim I was part of the conspiracy to lie to the court martial.

I couldn't believe it. Those GIs were smarter than I. They really had set me up. After much thought and soul searching, I did nothing. Was I right? To this day I'm not sure about that decision, but I learned a valuable lesson: Don't trust your client or his witnesses to tell the truth; they may lie. Dig out the facts. Find the truth.

One other charge that was scheduled for trial related to homosexual conduct in the military. Two soldiers that I will call Joe and Mike were caught engaging in a homosexual act. The commanding officer of their unit — they worked in the mess hall — brought charges against them. I served as defense counsel.

Prior to the trial, I located an Army directive, which stated that homosexuals were to be examined and treated at a military hospital and then transferred to a different military unit. I brought this information to the attention of the group commander. The charges were dropped. Joe and Mike were shipped off to a military general hospital in Calcutta.

End of case?

Not quite.

In a week, the hospital returned both soldiers to their original company unit. The personnel there all knew of the homosexual activity. These defendants were subject to derision, to laughter and to being the target of many jokes. This was a sad commentary on the treatment of these soldiers.

When I look back, my life in the military is like a separate arm from the rest of my life as a civilian.

One more important incident happened before I left the military. While on terminal leave back in the United States, still under military pay, I met Frances "Fritzie" Reisler of Clinton, Iowa, who was then serving in the Navy as a WAVE. I had said to myself I would never date or marry a servicewoman. I was wrong.

And so my back-to-civilian life story continues.

— CHAPTER 6 —

My Return

After four years of military service overseas, I came home to Eveleth in the spring of 1946 wearing the ruptured duck emblem denoting a returning World War II veteran. My reunion was bittersweet because few of my former friends, both guys and gals, had remained in Eveleth. Some had married, while others had left for jobs in other communities. But my spirits were lifted with the aroma of Ma's superb home cooking and the prospect of fishing, camping and playing tennis all summer long.

In spite of the fact that I knew the law school would start a summer session in June, I was reluctant to go back at that time. I was just having too much fun. In the end, good judgment won over my lethargy and good-time attitude. At the last minute, I returned to the University of Minnesota campus that summer and commenced my final year as a law student.

As always, adequate housing was the first hurdle, and returning veterans, who enrolled at the university in droves, exacerbated an already difficult situation. With the war-time hiatus on building resulting from rent controls and the like, there was simply little private housing available. I summoned the help of my friend and Navy war veteran, Kenneth Simon, of Virginia, Minnesota (Iron Range town). We were able to secure rooms in the Delta Upsilon Pi fraternity house. Apparently there was no objection to Simon and me, both Jewish students, rooming at the house during the summer, even though Delta Upsilon Pi would not admit Jewish students as fraternity members.

With the university campus bulging at the seams with returning

GIs, the law school administration found it necessary to run classes year round to accommodate the swelling ranks of new freshman law students and those of us who returned to school to complete our degrees. David Brink, one of our freshman classmates of B's, returned to school after military service with the Navy. Another friend, Orville Freeman, had suffered a disfiguring facial wound and attendant speech problems. Orville had served with the Marines and had seen considerable combat action.

In the summer of 1946, with four years of military service and the maturity that it fostered in me, I was determined to become a student-scholar. In this, my last year of law school, I sought the prized goal of achieving high marks and acquiring a good legal education. As a result of studying with much greater effectiveness and efficiency, most of my summer session grades were A's.

Although I maintained a heavy class load during the fall quarter, I made arrangements to work on the *Minnesota Law Review,* which I had always wanted to do. I eventually wrote and published two case notes for the journal. That work enriched my experience in research and writing, and the skills acquired then proved very valuable to me later in practicing law and also in my work as a federal appellate judge.

While I was deep into my studies that fall, another individual entered the university who would, in quick order, change my life dramatically and forever. Her name was Frances "Fritzie" Reisler, whom I had become acquainted with previously during a trip to Chicago. She had recently arrived in Minneapolis to pursue an education, or that is what I had thought. Yet, I had the feeling she had an ulterior motive—to heat up our somewhat cooled romance.

I met Fritzie in May in Chicago while visiting friends and relatives. I had arranged a meeting and a romantic time, I thought, with a former Eveleth girlfriend, Jean Eddy. However, those plans went awry. Jean had become engaged to Captain Walter Crowl, also in the military, just before coming to Chicago. The Bright-Eddy romance was not to be. (That was my version of three strikes and you are out).

Fritzie was stationed at Great Lakes Naval Station, in the Chicago area. My sister, who was best friends with Fritzie's mother, asked me to call Fritzie and take her out. Thus began an up and down, off and on romance that ended on the up side.

In the fall of 1946, all students wishing to attend the University of

Minnesota for the first time needed to achieve high scores on the qualification exams. I surmised that Fritzie would have a difficult time in that nonresidents were given no priority, unless they had military service and made the grade on the qualification test. Although a former WAVE, she still needed a high score. The night before her scheduled test, my roommate Kenneth Simon and I took Fritzie out partying, and made sure she had quite a bit of booze to drink. In the back of my mind, I think I was hoping she would not qualify for admittance to the university, and thus I would not have to worry about an immediate marriage and could conduct my romance with her a little more casually and with distance between us. To my surprise, she did very well on her examination, enrolled in the university and proved to be one very bright lady.

I did not know it at the time, but my fate was sealed. Our romance blossomed and by November, Fritzie and I were engaged. She subsequently left school to plan our wedding. At twenty-seven, I felt too young to marry. Nevertheless, the twenty-two-year-old former Navy WAVE from Clinton, Iowa, became my wife on December 26, 1946.

I pressed on with the last of my law school courses in the early winter of 1947. David Brink and I had taken a course in administrative law from Professor Stephen Reisenfeldt, who spoke mixed guttural German with his English. His lectures were extremely difficult to follow and I often wondered whether I had learned anything from him. The day after our final examination, we met Reisenfeldt in the lobby of the law school. We inquired about our grades, but he said that he had not completed grading the papers. However, he did mention, much to our chagrin, that our fellow classmate William Mussman had written a superb exam and had been awarded an A for his efforts. The following day we were pleasantly surprised to learn from Reisenfeldt that we had also earned A's on our exams.

Three months later, at the end of the winter quarter in March of 1947, I graduated from law school. My mother and new bride attended graduation ceremonies at Northrop Memorial Auditorium on campus. Upon reflection, my experience there made me realize that what is important in education and in life is the *finish*, not necessarily the *beginning*. I began my law school career with good grades, dropped to a lower class rank due to overconfidence, improved somewhat during my third year, and then finally achieved an A average in my senior year.

Those who graduated with me or shortly thereafter had begun their law studies in 1939, interrupted their education to serve in the military and returned to finish what they had started several years earlier. Almost all did well in the legal profession. Some became great lawyers, some served in the government, others became judges, and still others became great law teachers. Throughout my time at the University of Minnesota, I had established and nurtured friendships with many of them, and those friendships have remained with and sustained me all of these long years.

— CHAPTER 7 —

Last Test and First Job

Upon graduation from the University of Minnesota Law School in March 1947, I faced what I considered a tremendous hurdle — passing the Minnesota state bar examination.

Preparation required resurrecting my old class notes, some dating to my freshman year back in 1939. The gap of eight years was like learning the law all over again. The rigors of renewed study were further complicated by the fact that some pages of my notebooks were incomprehensible, due in large measure to studying late at night and then the next day falling asleep in class. These bad study habits had now caught up with me.

After the hustle and bustle of the Twin Cities, I felt I needed a quiet place to prepare for the exam. So Fritzie and I packed up our 1946 four-door Plymouth sedan, which we had lovingly named "Matilda," and headed home to Eveleth, where I began the arduous task of filling my mind with the law. To make matters worse, I developed a serious cold and was forced to retreat to my bed. I can still clearly recall the law books strewn among my bed covers as I perused the pages of constitutional law, torts and property rights with handkerchief in hand to wipe away the sniffles.

Anxiety was my closest friend the morning of the bar exam, which I took in St. Paul along with three hundred or so other aspiring attorneys. Much to my surprise, I not only passed the exam, but achieved the second highest score of all those who sat for it. My brother Joe, the family's first lawyer, made arrangements to have me sworn in before the Minnesota Supreme Court in a separate ceremony, which he attended. That event has been lovingly stored in my heart and mind all of these years.

If the bar exam was rigorous, the law firm interviews that proceeded my journey into the legal profession were as remarkable — both good and bad. Just prior to graduation, I interviewed with a lawyer from the Lewis and Hammer firm in Duluth. Toward the end of the interview, I was asked my religious affiliation, to which I replied, "I'm Jewish."

Following a couple additional questions regarding my faith and that of my wife, the interviewer commented: "We do a lot of insurance litigation and the insurance company lawyers do not like Jewish lawyers." The conversation and the painfully obvious anti-Semitism of Mr. Hammer hit me like a wet towel across the face. In spite of all of the egalitarian efforts of World War II and its aftermath, racial bias remained alive and well in America's legal profession.

The aftershocks of my first interview compelled me to make application to a Jewish firm, Brill and Maslon in Minneapolis. The senior partner, Samuel Maslon, had served as a law clerk to U.S. Supreme Court Justice Louis D. Brandeis. I was interviewed by "Bud" Brill, a fraternity brother and son of partner Josiah Brill. I knew I wouldn't face discrimination on account of my religion. Although my faith was not an issue, Brill conducted the interview with a tinge of arrogance and with indifference to my salary needs, which he deemed were non-negotiable, as I remember the conversation:

Bud: "We have an opening. We will pay 150 dollars per month for a lawyer. There are no guarantees that the lawyer will ever be a member of the firm, just an employee."

Me: "I'm married. I can't support a wife on 150 dollars per month."

Bud: "That's your problem."

Needless to say, I would not have accepted an offer had one been made. Too, with roots deep in the small towns on the Iron Range, the Twin Cities seemed to me just too big. Perhaps, I needed to practice law in a smaller place.

Shortly thereafter, I learned of an opening in a labor law office in Duluth. Following the death of Henry Paul, his partner Sidney Kaner, of Paul and Kaner, became the sole remaining partner. This firm successfully practiced labor law with labor unions as clients. Although the interview went well, I lost some interest in the position upon learning that Paul's widow controlled the labor union business in Duluth, and she may have had ties to the local Communist Party. I had some reservations about practicing law too close to home as Duluth is only fifty-three miles from Eveleth. Fritzie expressed similar concerns at taking up residence so near her new in-laws. Furthermore, we had contemplated an extended trip west to seek our fortunes perhaps in Denver, Phoenix or even Portland.

Just prior to our intended departure west, Everett Fraser, dean of the law school, called and inquired whether I had been placed. When I said no, he invited me to the law school to interview with a lawyer from Fargo, who was looking for a prospective trial lawyer. Fortunately for me, I had been recommended by my former trial practice professor, Professor Cherry.

I recall that experience as though it occurred yesterday rather than more than sixty-five years ago. Upon my arrival at the law school interview room, a tall, slender, severe-looking man by the name of Mart R. Vogel greeted me. Mart wore a checked gray suit, belted in the back, pince-nez glasses perched on his nose. His black Homburg hat graced the table. My immediate thought was, "Boy, is this guy conservative! I'll never survive the first round."

I was wrong about Mart, and quickly re-learned that one cannot tell a book by its cover nor a man's character and personality from his apparel.

In the course of the interview, Vogel indicated he was with a three-member firm in Fargo and was looking for a young man interested in trial work. He also mentioned that his firm did a great deal of insurance litigation.

Recounting immediately in my mind the verbal exchange in the recent Lewis and Hammer interview concerning my religious affiliation, I quickly proffered, "You know I'm Jewish."

Vogel replied, "What difference does that make?" In all the long, legal years from 1947 to the year of Mart Vogel's death in 2005, it never made any difference at all.

Following the interview at the law school, I began to weigh the pros and cons of practicing with a Jewish firm such as Sidney Kaner in Duluth or with a gentile firm like Mart Vogel's in Fargo. In need of practical advice, I visited Fraser at the law school.

After I presented my potential career paths, as I saw them, Fraser expressed his sentiments on religious prejudice in a most emphatic manner: "I'm sick and tired of Jewish law graduates going into Jewish law firms, and gentile law graduates going with gentile firms. Myron, if you get a chance to break this cycle and go with a gentile law firm, do it."

I add a delightful tale which occurred during my conversation with Fraser. For background, the following rule applied:

Smoking was forbidden in the law school but not outside. The dean smoked a smelly pipe, but outside the building. In our conversation, I mentioned to the dean that my wife, Fritzie, who smoked, had asked him for a light for her cigarette one day. Fritzie had been waiting for me in the entryway to the building.

Fritzie told me she had obtained a match from a person who looked like the janitor. When she described that person to me, I almost fainted. She had described Fraser.

The light-giver had said to Fritzie, "I'll give you a light, young lady, but smoke outside."

When I related the story to Fraser, who looked and acted like the dour Scotsman that he was, he leaned back in his chair and literally shook with laughter. I returned to the job search and decision.

In late April, the Vogel firm requested a second interview, and Fritzie and I traveled west to Fargo. There, we interviewed with senior partner Charles Wattam and Mart's brother, Philip Vogel. Most of the interview was conducted by Philip, who eventually extended an offer to me, saying, "Myron, we would like you to come to work for us. If you do and it works out, we want to make you a partner."

When asked my salary needs, I replied with a shaking voice, "Is two hundred per month OK?" He agreed, and gave me a week or so to think about it.

When making monumental decisions in one's life, fishing on a peaceful lake far from the city lights can bring focus to such issues. After touring Fargo and finding it to our liking, and discovering from the locals that the Vogel firm had a great reputation, Fritzie and I headed out for the water at Lake Vermillion, some forty miles from Eveleth. Between baiting hooks and frying fish, we talked about a thousand things and had a wonderful time together. In early May, I accepted the offer to join the Vogel firm, and two weeks later Fritzie and I started our new life together in Fargo.

Did I make the right choice? Time would tell.

— CHAPTER 8 —

New Lawyer Fargo, Here I Come

In these next few chapters, I shall attempt to capsulate twenty-one years as a lawyer. That task is a daunting one because my aim in this autobiography is to explain some of my experiences that have played a role in my service as a judge.

We start at the beginning. The date I believe is May 27, 1947. Fritzie and I, loaded down with five or six suitcases containing all of our belongings, roll into the bustling city of Fargo driving Matilda, our 1946 Plymouth sedan. We check into the Fargo's best hotel, the Gardner. The desk clerk who registered us advises that we can stay in the hotel only five days because of the housing shortage due to WWII rent control.

We could not find a place to rent in the five days we stayed at the Gardner. I recall that our first room for two days had no toilet. In the next room for three days, we did have a toilet, but no clothes closet. We hung the clothes from wire strung along the wall.

John Bennison, a friend of Phil Vogel, came to our rescue and found a place for us to live. Professor Hunter, from the North Dakota Agricultural College in Fargo, agreed to rent us his fully furnished apartment on North Broadway during the summer while we continued seeking housing for the longer term.

The rental worked out well with one small problem: Our bedroom contained twin beds rather than a double bed. As newlyweds, Fritzie and

I enjoyed sleeping together. We solved the problem by attaching the twin beds together with one of my belts.

One Sunday morning, the belt broke and the beds fell apart, making a loud noise. Hunter knocked. When I opened the door, he commented, "I knew that would happen sometime!"

After a few months, we did find an apartment nearby. It consisted of a fairly spacious living room, a small kitchen, a bath and a closet in which we would store and pull out a double bed on wheels. The bed would be kept in the closet as it could be raised to an upright position. We managed. The rent was thirty-five dollars, but that was all I could afford on my two-hundred-dollar monthly salary.

The firm, Wattam, Vogel and Vogel, occupied an office space on the third floor of the building known as the Edwards Building, at 20½ Broadway (the ½ meant upstairs). The main floor provided space for a tavern plus a men's store operated by Sam Stern. A brother of Sam's, Bill, was a bank president and the leading Republican in North Dakota, serving as a Republican National Committeeman for this state. Another brother, Edward, served the federal government in Washington, D.C. Bill became my good friend and, believe it or not, a valued adviser to me eleven years later when I became Democratic chairman for Cass County.

Charlie Wattam occupied a corner office with a view looking east to Broadway, Fargo's principal business street, and looking north at NP (for Northern Pacific Railroad) Avenue. The brass spittoons in Charlie's office were very bright gold-colored receptacles. Charlie chewed a cigar and spat in the spittoon. I never saw him smoke.

As I recall, Phil Vogel worked in an office next to Charlie, also overlooking NP Avenue; Mart's office was next to the south, overlooking Broadway. I was next to him to the south, also overlooking Broadway. The offices of Phil, Mart and me were fairly roomy but hardly plush—no carpeting, linoleum on the floor and shades, not blinds, on the windows.

I did inquire about a coiled heavy rope in my office and Mart advised me, "That is your fire escape."

The firm kept a very complete library of law books, legal materials, etc., in the rear section. Three secretaries occupied a square space between the lawyers' offices and the law library.

There I started my career.

As a recent law graduate, I knew a lot of legal principles, but believe me, I had much to learn. I learned, and learned fast. Mart served as my principal mentor. One early important skill I learned from Mart: how to get the facts.

The firm did much in the way of insurance work, representing mostly companies that provided automobile liability insurance. Automobile accidents generated much of the firm's business. The lawyers investigated and adjusted claims, served as local legal advisors to insurers, and also represented the insured in litigation.

The first step required investigation. Who became the investigator? Myron!

How do you investigate? I needed to get the facts from the parties and witnesses. That meant writing statements of facts obtained from interviews with those persons.

Mart took me out with him on an interview with a witness. He asked questions and wrote down in narrative form the story given by the witness. The statement, as written by Mart, was then provided to the witness, who was asked to sign it, including this legend: "I have read the above statement of ___ pages and it is true."

After some practice, I could write legibly and with accuracy as the person spoke. Those statements, police reports, photographs of the scene, pictures taken by persons investigating, and our pictures formed the foundation for decisions, settlement conferences and, later, litigation.

I might add that both Mart and Phil maintained an open-door policy for me to obtain their counsel and advice. I was a very lucky young lawyer, which brings me to an early story.

I accompanied Mart to the early call of the calendar at the local Cass County Courthouse, as well as the calendar at the Clay County Courthouse located just across the Red River, in Moorhead, Minnesota. The calendar call scheduled cases for trial. The Vogel firm practices heavily in both jurisdictions. At the "call," the lawyers and judge made tentative dates for when the pending cases would be set for trial.

An early call in Moorhead I remember well. An older lawyer, Edgar Sharp, introduced himself and we had a friendly conversation. During our talk, Sharp said, "Myron, you should have contacted me for a job. Our firm name could have been Sharp and Bright." He laughed and we became good friends.

Time passed. I tried many cases in my first five years. I called that period my learning time and I had plenty to learn. I won only a few and lost many. One can learn much by losing.

We'll start with my first case as a lawyer.

I don't remember their names, but there were sixteen of them. They occupied an apartment building in downtown Fargo. The landlord, to whom I'll give the name Tony Lazar (not his real name), had obtained an eviction order from the justice of the peace. The eviction order stated that those tenants must vacate the premises for nonpayment of rent. With rent control, landlords could not raise rents of their existing tenants, but could get relief legally (or perhaps illegally) by payments under the table from new renters.

The tenants I represented were poor. Some retired, some disabled and some with low-paying jobs. They gave me a simple and straightforward story. They had offered the rent money to Tony, who refused to take it. Tony then got a good lawyer, James Conmy, and told him the tenants did not pay their rent—true, but not the whole story. Tony had rejected their payments.

Maybe I could get justice for these people.

I took the case with no money down. I looked up the law and appealed the eviction order of the justice of the peace to the Cass County District Court. The district judge, John Pollock, set the case for an early trial. I arranged for the required rentals to be deposited in the court's registry.

I looked into its facts and felt Tony would lie on the stand about the tender to him of rent. On a hunch, I contacted the North Dakota State Crime Bureau to learn if Tony, now a successful owner of rental property as well as an owner and operator of a tavern, might just have a criminal record.

Bingo! I connected. Tony had been convicted in 1928 as a bootlegger for illegally bringing liquor into the United States. He had served as an armed guard on the truck on which the liquor had traveled from Canada to the United States. In the 1920s, the Volstead Act banned importation, manufacturing or sale of alcoholic beverages in the United States.

Well, I could not wait for the trial date. Mart Vogel, my mentor, gave me some sage advice for this trial: "Tell the jury it's your first case. You're bound to win."

The trial date arrived. My sixteen clients, clean and neatly dressed, attended. I assisted in picking the jury. The trial proceeded. My witnesses all swore that each tried to pay his or her rent and that Tony would not take their check or cash.

My position was clear. I had told the jury in an opening statement that tender of payment of rent by a renter amounted to payment of the rent.

Tony got on the stand and denied everything.

I rose to cross examine Tony. I said, "Have you ever been convicted of a felony, in particular bootlegging in 1928?"

His face turned red and he couldn't speak. Finally, he choked out an almost silent yes.

I repeated, "You said *yes*." Tony nodded.

The cross-examination was over.

In redirect, Conmy established that Tony had paid his debt to society.

The testimony was over. Time for motions to protect the record as I believed my clients had established tender as a matter of law. Thus they could not be evicted, regardless of any contrary finding by the jury. I moved the jury to direct a verdict for the tenants.

Conmy then also moved for a directed verdict for his client. He sandbagged me on a practice issue of which was I was unaware. The rule at that time in North Dakota courts was that if both parties moved for directed verdict, the issue became a question of law for the judge to decide.

So the judge dismissed the jury. I felt like I had let my clients down. Judge Pollock said, "I'll decide this case."

Although the jury was with me, I didn't know much about the judge. I thought next time I'd better know everything about the law as it applied to my case.

As in a movie, everything came out all right. The judge rendered a written decision in my clients' favor — they could not be evicted as long as the rent was paid. Tony either had to accept the rent if tendered or lose the rent. The renters were saved.

My clients took up a collection and raised sixty-five dollars. My fee! Not very much but all they could afford. The joy of winning and getting a good result for deserving people amounted to a great reward for me.

In the fall of 1947, with ongoing litigation and a busy schedule, I usually worked two or three evenings at the office. My absences, particularly at night, became a sore spot for Fritzie. One evening, she said to me,

"Myron, today I visited with our landlord, Margaret Benson Hawkins. Her father, now a judge, practiced law in Bottineau and made a good living. Margaret told me that her father went to work at 9 o'clock in the morning, came home at noon for lunch, took a little nap after lunch, and then returned to work at 2:00 p.m. He worked at his law business until 4 o'clock in the afternoon and then returned home and he never brought home any briefcase of work."

Fritzie paused, looked me straight in the eye and exclaimed, "Why can't you be like that!" I shut up.

A few months passed. I continued working at night at the law office and at home. One evening I picked up *The Forum,* the local daily newspaper, which had published a news story about Judge Asmunder Benson, Margaret's father. The gist of the article was that the Supreme Court of North Dakota had reversed Judge Benson in ten of eleven cases on appeal. Showing her the story, I said, "Fritzie, that's why I work at night."

As part of work, in the evening after Fritzie and I had eaten supper, I would tell my wife the facts of a pending case. I would have her become one of the witnesses for the other side and then I would commence the cross-examination.

After about the third session, we quit. "You're driving me crazy," she said.

The night law work continued as it has through my entire legal career. There are not enough hours ever to know everything one should know as a lawyer and judge. My crucial first five years as a lawyer served as my learning time. I was not a great success. I remember trying and losing cases in Grand Forks, North Dakota, and in Crookston, Minnesota, as well as in Fargo and Moorhead.

I took these losses hard and at one time told Fritzie maybe I wasn't cut out to be a trial lawyer.

By losing cases, I learned. Particularly, I learned how to persuade the jury. I had assumed a lawyer should tell a jury what it should do. That technique did not work. Rather, I learned, by talking to jurors who had sat on my cases and in trying varying approaches of jury persuasion that jurors need to be led, not told what to do. Show them the road. Let them decide.

Statements such as "is that reasonable?" or, after mentioning an important fact, "what do you think?" often got the jury agreeing with me.

After about three years of trying many cases, things began to turn my way and I began winning my lawsuits.

Here were my conclusions: If on analysis I had a forty percent chance of winning, the case was one for settlement. I could win almost all cases considered fifty or fifty-five percent against me.

In the following years, I tried scores of cases in North Dakota and Minnesota, in both the state courts and federal courts.

Because I remembered many of those in my work as a federal judge and also in my years as a law professor teaching trial practice to law students, I mention some of them in the next chapter. Those experiences have served me well.

— CHAPTER 9 —

On Being a Trial Lawyer

As I recollect my twenty-one years as a lawyer, I'm reminded of a conversation between Fritzie and me in June of 1965. My family, Fritzie, son Joshua Robert, age nine, and daughter Dinah Ann, age thirteen, were in my white Chrysler four-door sedan driving from Fargo to Washington, D.C., for a family vacation.

Somewhere on the Pennsylvania Turnpike, here is the conversation:

Fritzie speaks, "Myron, when we get to Washington, why don't you ask Quentin [U.S. Senator Quentin Burdick, a very close friend] about being a federal judge?"

Myron responds, "What in the hell do I want a judgeship for. I am having too much fun as a trial lawyer."

Fritzie retorts, "Listen, I want a live husband, not a dead trial lawyer."

That conversation represents my great love of being a trial lawyer.

I worked very hard as a trial lawyer and wanted to win my case whether in a civil case the amount in controversy was five thousand or fifty thousand dollars. I did a complete job of investigating and preparing for trial. I loved the exultation of winning; it was a high; but I hated the sad feeling, the low that went with losing.

I also served as an appellate lawyer before the Supreme Court of North Dakota in scores of cases and argued one appeal in the Court of Appeals for the Eighth Circuit. In addition, I briefed a second case in that Eighth Circuit court — my partner Philip Vogel argued that one.

Inasmuch as I have now served on that Eighth Circuit for forty-five years, it might be of some interest to know that I lost in both appeals in that court.

I remember well one of my early cases in the North Dakota courts. Our firm represented the insurance carrier for the trucks operated by the Great Northern Railway. In the summer of 1947, Mart Vogel gave me a file and said defend the case, which related to a truck-car accident. The car driver sued the Great Northern for damages.

So I went up to defend this case in a very rural county. The whole thing was a hoot.

The plaintiff's lawyer, who also served as a prosecuting attorney in the county, had never tried a case in his ten years of practice. The county courthouse had been taken over for other business of the county and state, so the county had rented a room in a downtown building to use as a courtroom.

This was my first case outside of Fargo. Somehow, the other lawyer and I got a jury picked and tried the case. The judge, too, was very inexperienced. We had a fun time. Not much in the way of damages was claimed and I won.

I recall with some chagrin a case tried sometime before 1955 in the federal court in Fargo. I don't recall the name of the case, but the circumstances have remained etched in my memory, mainly because of the conduct of my opposing lawyer, Lewis Oehlert, a very sharp and able trial lawyer from the firm of Nilles, Oehlert and Nilles, a leading law firm in Fargo.

The lawsuit related to a two-car accident with injuries to the drivers of each automobile. Oehlert led in the race to the federal courthouse door and his client, a Fargo photographer, brought a civil action for injuries. Let's call the plaintiff Bonham, represented by Oehlert, and the defendant Burley, whom I represented in defense and with a counterclaim for his injuries.

I learned plenty. For one, don't take the truth for granted. Make sure that your witness will be credible before the jury. My witness, a North Dakota highway patrolman, testified that Bonham had admitted at the scene that the accident was his fault. But he denied the statement at trial.

Oehlert convinced the jury that the highway patrolman didn't remember much in the way of details about the accident scene, the weather and myriad irrelevant details. His strategy worked. The jury denied the claims of both parties.

I mention three cases that taught me that persistence pays and that a lawyer does not give up or surrender when the lawyer knows he or she is in the right.

Early in my career, in 1952, a young man, age twenty, I'll call him John Johnson, a veteran of the U.S. Army, came to me with a sad tale. He lost part of his hand in an accident with a saw while working as a carpenter's helper. He was eligible for workers compensation benefits, but he had received nothing.

A local company called Broadway Investment Company had figured out a scheme to avoid paying premiums to the state of North Dakota for workers compensation coverage. Neat deal! Broadway Investment had its four carpenter employees, including Johnson, sign a contract form calling them independent contractors. Thus, as independent contractors, Broadway did not need to submit premiums to the compensation fund for them. I claimed the contract masked the truth: Johnson and others were mere employees and Johnson was entitled to workers compensation benefits.

I brought a proceeding before the North Dakota Workers Compensation Bureau alleging Broadway Investment served as an uninsured employer and should be required to pay benefits.

I won.

Broadway appealed to the state District Court of Cass County.

I lost.

I took an appeal to the North Dakota Supreme Court.

I lost.

But the Supreme Court in some language in its opinion stated that one Mr. Mikkelson, who served as a supervisor for Broadway Investment, could be the employer.

I followed that suggestion and again brought proceedings to collect compensation before the North Dakota Workers Compensation Bureau. I finally won.

Justice can be done. It took seven years, 1952-1959.[5]

A second case with a similar lesson was *Dick v. New York Life Insurance Company* (1959), which ended up in the U.S. Supreme Court. My partner Phil Vogel served as the lead lawyer in that litigation. All of us in the firm were working with Philip in the saga of that litigation. That was some case.

Briefly, a farmer, Lawrence Dick of Ransom County, North Dakota, was found dead in an outbuilding on his farm. He had been killed by two blasts from his double-barreled shotgun. The coroner's inquest called it suicide.

The Dick family, wife and children, all said, "Lawrence Dick would never commit suicide. He loved his life."

No motive or reason for suicide ever surfaced.

Dick owned a life insurance policy written by New York Life Insurance Company with death benefits of seventy-five hundred dollars, but double indemnity added another seventy-five hundred dollars for accidental death. It wasn't the money that counted with the Dick survivors, but the shame of having his death labeled as suicide.

A colleague lawyer friend, Don Holand of Lisbon, served as the Dick family attorney and brought Phil Vogel into the controversy.

Vogel first attacked the coroner's ruling that Dick had committed suicide, and he succeeded in vacating that ruling.

Next, he brought an action in the Federal District Court in Fargo against New York Life for double-indemnity benefits of fifteen thousand dollars as an accidental death. He demanded and received a trial by jury.

The insurance company had offered to pay regular death benefits of seventy-five hundred dollars and, as a defense to double indemnity, asserted that suicide caused Dick's death and double indemnity did not cover suicide because it was not an accidental death.

In the trial, the Dick family members testified to Dick's love of life. A shotgun expert testified to some defect in that gun's trigger mechanism.

In his argument to the jury, Phil asserted a theory that the defect caused the first shot from the gun that injured Dick and that as he swung around from the blast, the trigger mechanism caused a second round to kill him.

The jury ruled in favor of the Dick family. But New York Life appealed that adverse ruling and judgment to the Court of Appeals for the Eighth Circuit.

That court reversed. Judge Sanborn wrote in part that a discharge of a single shotgun shell might be accidental, but not two. That was a low blow. The only avenue of possible relief was to ask for review in the U.S. Supreme Court.

The Dick case was not a very important case for Supreme Court review. It really involved a simple insurance claim governed by the law of the state of North Dakota and not any broader national problem.

Vogel was not deterred. He wrote a powerful, but succinct petition to the Supreme Court to take the case.

The Supreme Court had never before taken such a case for review and, I might add, never since. But miracle of miracles! Yes. The Supreme Court granted review. It reversed the Eighth Circuit and reinstated the double-indemnity award.

We were overjoyed in the law office.

It has been said that the then-chief justice, Earl Warren, who wrote the opinion, had a soft spot in his heart for "widows, orphans and railroad workers." His father had worked on a railroad.

Oh, yes, a sidelight. Vogel told me this vignette:

As he and Holand left the Supreme Court building, two men in priestly collars stopped them. One said to Vogel, "Did you just argue that shotgun death case?" When Vogel said yes, the priest said, "We'll pray for you." Prayers worked!

The lessons:

1. In the quest for justice, never give up.
2. Prayer may help.

I also wrote an article about the case for the *Journal of the Supreme Court Historical Society.* ("The Case of William Dick," June 2010).

The Dick case and its result gave me hope for justice in another case in which an appeals court "done me wrong." That case title was *Anderson v. Schreiner.*

This involved a horrible accident. Kenneth Anderson, his sister, and Kenneth's wife, while driving south on a rural highway in Sargent County, North Dakota, had a collision at an intersection with a westbound automobile driven by Alfred Schreiner. Schreiner obviously entered the intersection at a very high speed, did not stop for the stop sign, and the force of the collision knocked Anderson's car into the air for fifty to seventy-five feet, where it landed in a farm field bordering the intersection. A young lady passenger in the Schreiner car was killed. Anderson, his sister, and his wife all sustained serious injuries.

The case that I tried related only to the injuries to Kenneth Anderson, who at that time was age twenty-two and a student at one of the universities in North Dakota.

This was a very hard-fought case, with the defense claiming that Anderson was partly at fault for not seeing Schreiner's speeding car and thereafter not slowing or stopping to avoid the accident.

The jury decided for the plaintiff-driver, Anderson, and awarded damages of twenty thousand dollars — a sizable award for 1958. The defense appealed to the North Dakota Supreme Court. I argued the appeal and was very confident of success.

But no such luck. The Supreme Court unanimously determined that Anderson was guilty of contributory negligence as a matter of law and directed that Anderson's claim be dismissed. I was aghast at the result and immediately began working on a petition for rehearing, assisted by a law student intern, Roger Cohen, who worked with the firm that summer. Cohen was attending Harvard Law School.

I asked Cohen to research the law. He did and came back to me and said, "Myron, I think they (the Supreme Court justices) are right."

"They are wrong," I replied.

I wrote a strong petition for rehearing, emphasizing that a driver on a highway protected by stop signs should not have to anticipate a high-speed car driving into the intersection. When Anderson may have looked to the left, the Schreiner car was probably not even near the intersection because of the high speed at which it was moving (I estimated as high as ninety miles per hour).

Unbelievable. It almost never happens. The Supreme Court granted a rehearing and a re-argument.

This time, I was well prepared, carefully explained all the facts to the court, and used a good bit of demonstrative evidence such as photographs.

I remember, even today, more than fifty years later, one judge asking me, "You mean there was a stop sign there protecting Anderson?"

"Yes, sir."

The court had vacated its first opinion. This time, the court got it right, affirmed in *Anderson v. Schreiner* (1959).

The lesson for my life: If I think I'm right, don't give up. Secondly, you can't be sure the judges on appeal know all the facts.

I had many successes and a few losses in the scores of cases that I tried in the ten years after the *Anderson-Schreiner* experience.

I mention some significant cases discussed in my personal data questionnaire submitted to the Justice Department in connection with my nomination to serve as a U.S. circuit judge.

In 1958, a young friend of mine, as a member of the North Dakota Legislature, voted certain benefits for the then-governor, including an appropriation to build a new governor's mansion. In 1960, this young man, William L. Guy, was himself elected governor. His right to hold office was challenged on grounds that, as a legislator, he had voted an increase in the emoluments (salary or benefits) in the governor's office contrary to the state constitution. Mart Vogel and I represented Governor Guy on an original quo warranto proceeding before the North Dakota Supreme Court. I wrote the brief for the case and the Supreme Court sustained Guy's right to office. I take great pride in this matter because I feel that Guy has truly been one of the outstanding governors in the history of the state.[6]

Leading to another memorable case, on July 31, 1965, William Bry Newgard, a patient with a mental illness under the supervision of the Veterans Administration Hospital at Fort Mead, South Dakota, committed the brutal killing by a firearm of his wife, Eloise A. Newgard, at Detroit Lakes, Minnesota. Three young children lost their mother, as well as the services of the father, who was later convicted in Minnesota of first-degree murder.

The Newgards lived in Fargo. As I indicated, the Veterans Administration hospital was located in South Dakota and the homicide occurred in Minnesota. Our firm brought a federal torts claim action against the United States of America, and this was tried in the U. S. District Court for the District of North Dakota during July of 1967. In a trial that involved doctors, psychiatrists and psychologists who appeared as witnesses for the plaintiff and defendant, the trial judge determined that the United States and the Veterans Administration facility were negligent in their custodial care of William Bry Newgard and awarded the Newgard estate two hundred thousand dollars.

This was the largest award for wrongful death in the history of North Dakota, and the case involved very significant points of law in multi-state torts. The North Dakota wrongful death statute was held to apply under the "Most Significant Contacts Conflicts of Law Rule" rather than the application of "Lew Loci Delicti" (place of the incident).[7]

In another case, a young man in his early twenties saw a quick road to success by selling life and health and accident insurance for an Iowa company doing business in North Dakota. In his efforts to maintain a high standing with his state sales manager, Irwin Warfield wrote a number of false applications and submitted forged checks to his company. No policyholder sustained any damage, but his company paid commissions on business that was not actually ever in force. The United States indicted the young man on thirteen counts of interstate transportation of forged documents.

The jury returned a verdict of guilty on approximately nine counts. In his sentence, trial judge Ronald Davies gave Warfield no prison time but a chance to wipe out the conviction by good behavior for several years. Warfield rehabilitated himself following his conviction and became a good citizen.

The case was of some satisfaction to me, not because of the conviction, but because of the result of this conviction. The conviction became vacated by reason of Warfield's good behavior following the conviction.[8]

But let me now return to Lewis Oehlert and my revenge.

Let's set the scene: An auto accident occurred between two cars going north on North Dakota Highway 32, some five miles north of Lisbon.

Car #1, driven by a young lady we'll call Mary Jones, made a left turn into a driveway leading to a farmhouse.

Car #2, driven by a person we'll call James Olson, was traveling behind car #1 and when car #1 turned left into the driveway to a farm, car #2, in the process of trying to pass car #1, collided with #1. A passenger in car #2 riding in the front seat was thrown out of the car and sustained injuries, essentially a broken leg (femur) in three places. We'll name the passenger Nancy Worth, who was otherwise completely disabled from muscular dystrophy.

Worth retained Fargo lawyer Frank Knox, a fine advocate and my good friend. Representing the driver of car #1, I immediately agreed to pay fifty percent of any settlement reached and suggested to Knox that the lawyer for car #2, Louie Oehlert, be contacted to pay the other fifty percent. Frank and I agreed that a settlement of five thousand dollars would be fair.

Oehlert, who was nicknamed "Fair Lewie," would often say to a jury, "let's be fair." Yet his conduct as a trial lawyer reflected unfairness. Fair Lewie was a term of derision. Oehlert, on behalf of driver of car #2, James Olson, refused to pay even a penny.

Oehlert conceded that James may have been negligent but argued he wasn't liable for damages to Mary because of the protection afforded a driver of a car under the North Dakota guest law, which provides that a host driver (James Olson) would be liable to a guest (Nancy Worth) in the vehicle only if the host had been guilty of gross negligence in causing an accident. Gross meant great negligence. That presented a real hurdle for plaintiff Nancy suing a host driver for damages in North Dakota.

Knox and I hatched an arrangement. We agreed to try to show gross negligence, that is conduct approaching recklessness by Olson.

I knew we had him this time. Worth sealed the fate of Oehlert's client, Olson, by stating she could see the speedometer on Olson's car and it read sixty-five miles per hour, which was over the speed limit by ten miles per hour. The jury decided against both defendants. Olson was found guilty of gross negligence and my client, Mary Jones, was guilty of ordinary negligence. However, the award was small, less than five thousand dollars.

The lesson to me: Rascals in the law will get what's due.

Although Fair Lewie Oehlert did not fit my view of a fine lawyer, he did teach me a great lesson about adversaries in the law and trial preparation. The lesson is prepare, prepare and prepare!

I do add one other nontrial event. After "calling off" a collection agency for a lady who came to me at my office for advice (the bill collector was harassing the lady on account of her husband's bill) she then asked, "How much do I owe you?"

I said, "Nothing, it was a pleasure." Thereafter for many years, after moving to a city in Wisconsin, she sent me greetings every Christmas.

So, have some compassion for the oppressed.

Next, let's talk politics.

Goodbye Mike, Hello Judge: My Journey for Justice

SECTION TWO

— CHAPTER 10 —

Politics — the Beginning

Early in my legal career, I decided to not engage in political activity until I became well established as a lawyer. However, I did have an early experience in partisan politics shortly after returning from military service in the spring of 1946. When I was at home in Eveleth, an older friend by the name of Maurice "Muck" Levant came to see me.

Muck asked if I'd like to be an alternate delegate to the St. Louis County Republican Convention, to be held in Duluth.

While I had voted for Franklin Delano Roosevelt in the 1940 and 1944 elections, I did not consider myself aligned with any political party.

I thought for a moment, recalled that Harold Stassen, a Republican, had been a good Minnesota governor, and thought the convention experience could be a good one.

So I went to the party convention as a new Republican.

That affiliation did not last very long. Here's the scene: A Republican legislator from the Minnesota Iron Range city of Chisholm offered a resolution favoring the right of miners in Iron Range communities to join a union if they wished to do so. The legislator asserted that the owners and operators of the iron mines were imposing harsh working conditions in the mines. The resolution received a second. At that point, a delegate who everyone knew represented the mining ownership interests moved to table the resolution.

The motion to table is not debatable. The chairman called for a voice vote and the convention resoundingly voted aye. The resolution was tabled.

I favored the sentiment behind the resolution and concluded that the mining company controlled the Republican delegation. So I left the convention, and I lost my Republicanism.

In the spring of 1954, the Democrats were having an intra-party fight. One faction consisted of precinct committeemen or women representing Democrats who were loyal to David Kelly of Grand Forks. Kelly was the party's national committeeman for North Dakota. We called that faction the Irish Mafia. The other faction, led by Fargo lawyer P.W. "Bill" Lanier Jr., was made up of Democrats in Fargo who wanted to broaden the party base to win elections. Lanier believed the Kelly people were interested in patronage from the national Democratic Party but not in winning elections.

Lanier was a close friend of my law partners Mart and Phillip Vogel and a new friend to me. He asked me to run for precinct committeeman. This didn't sound like much of a task, so I said yes.

As I recall it, this election for precinct committeeman occurred during the primary election in the spring of 1954. I prepared an advertising election flier about myself to be delivered to the homes in my precinct, No. 21.

Did I win? No.

Did I lose? No.

Did I tie with my Kelly opponent? Yes.

The winner was to be decided by the flip of a coin. I didn't realize it then, but I know it now: That coin flip proved to be one of my life's most significant events, for it made possible a very big change in my life.

I won the toss. I became an official of the Democratic Party as a precinct committeeman. We found out that the Irish Mafia really was interested in winning elections and not just controlling the party. The factions amalgamated and peace seemed to reign.

Because of my position as an official of the Democratic Party, my life became entwined with Quentin Burdick, who became my close friend. Perhaps I would never have become a federal judge; perhaps Quentin Burdick would not have been U.S. congressman and then a U.S. senator.

So let us turn to the Burdick story and the interrelation of the lives of the Brights, including Fritzie, Quentin Burdick, his first wife, Marietta, and his second wife, Jocelyn.

― CHAPTER 11 ―

First Time I Saw Quentin Beginning of a Friendship

I shall never forget the first time that I saw Quentin Burdick. He was in the company of his beautiful wife, Marietta. The time was over a half century ago. I had just begun practicing law with the Wattam, Vogel and Vogel firm. The annual North Dakota Bar Association meeting came to Fargo, probably in August of 1947. Fritzie and I attended the yearly banquet of the Bar.

The crowd had gathered in the large Elks ballroom and I was sitting with Fritzie. In walked in one of the most beautiful couples I have ever seen. Marietta Burdick—tall, dark complexion, wearing all white with a white turban around her head and, with the accent of the white clothing, she looked like a real beauty, which she was. Quentin—at that time age thirty-nine, with the shock of wavy brown hair, strong jaw and handsome ruddy complexion—could have qualified as a movie actor. Indeed, I think every eye in that large assembly looked at Quentin and Marietta.

Quentin and Marietta Burdick, my partners Philip and Mart Vogel, their respective wives, Barbara and Lois, Dr. Gordon and Helen Pepple, and Fritzie and I were part of what one might call the "liberal crowd" of Fargo. In essence, we were frustrated Democrats living in a sea of Republicans that controlled all of the elective offices in the state and had done so for many years.

My contacts with Quentin Burdick from 1947 to about 1955 were relatively casual. In 1955, I was in Minot as local counsel. I was staying downtown at the Clarence Parker Hotel, and I ran into Chris Nathan, the adjuster for the Farmers Union Insurance Company. Burdick was the retained counsel for the Farmers Union Insurance Company and defended most of the lawsuits brought against them or against their insureds in the state of North Dakota. He was defending a lawsuit in the state court while I was trying a case in the federal court.

In the late afternoon or early evening, I ran into Nathan in the halls of the hotel. He said Burdick had been defending this lawsuit and he had fainted and was in bed. I went over to see Burdick in his hotel room, and gosh, he looked as white as a sheet. I really was concerned.

At that time, my good friend, M.L. "Bill" Bearman, lived in Minot. With Bearman's help, we arranged for Burdick to see a doctor friend of Bearman's. The doctor checked Burdick over and decided that while there was no medical emergency, he ought to return to Fargo. Burdick's problem related to high blood pressure. We arranged to get him on a late train out of Minot. From that time on, he and I became close friends.

I remember a New Year's Day party at the Burdick home. I can recall the event so clearly because of what happened to Fritzie. Burdick served a punch drink that tasted wonderful. Fritzie had about four or five, not knowing that the punch had been laced with pure grain alcohol. When the alcohol hit her, she almost collapsed, got really intoxicated. We laughed about that event because she had remarked to Marietta, "Oh, what a wonderful nonalcoholic drink."

In 1956, when Burdick ran for the U.S. Senate against Republican incumbent Milton R. Young, Fritzie's obligation, as a regional director supervisor, was to organize the precincts and to get out the vote.

My contribution to the campaign in 1956 revolved around raising some money for the party. Burdick had a lot of friends in Fargo and we were able to generate some funding for his campaign — not a lot, though. Burdick lost the election by a big margin, about fifty thousand votes. At that point, I really thought Burdick's political years would be over and he would concentrate on the law practice.

— CHAPTER 12 —

Nomination and Election to Congress—1958

Prior to the 1958 campaign, in order to get the party organized, Fritzie and I ran an ad in the local newspaper sometime in January or maybe a little later, asking for all interested Democrats to attend a meeting at the Cass County Courthouse. The local Democratic Party was somewhat in disarray. We compiled a list of interested people, which led up to an organization of some kind to attend the state party convention.

The Democrats held their state party convention in Bismarck to endorse candidates. About a day or two prior, Mart Vogel had said, "Myron, you better go to Bismarck to help Quentin out." So, the morning of the nominations for Congress, Helen Pepple, an active Democrat and a good friend, along with some others, got in my car and left very early in the morning in order to arrive in Bismarck by 9:00 a.m.

I got to Bismarck and talked to Burdick. We agreed I would make his nominating speech to secure him the Democratic Party's endorsement. Why me? Good question.

I made a nominating speech for Burdick, and it was carried live over WDAY-TV in Fargo. Fritzie, who was coming to Bismarck on the train, viewed the program somewhere in Jamestown. I can't remember the text, but somebody said it was wonderful. I think that somebody was Don Crothers, a very prominent Republican and a state legislator. But Burdick did not receive the Democratic Party endorsement, even with my nomination speech.

The Democrats had planned a big fundraising dinner on the evening after the convention. The main speaker was a very handsome, popular young senator from Massachusetts, John F. Kennedy (JFK). At that time, little did we know that he would be an influence in our lives and become a president of the United States.

The evening event was held in Bismarck. The Fargo delegation, including Fritzie, Helen Pepple, Barbara Lindell and others, were angry about Burdick not getting the party nomination. We decided we would desert the Democratic dinner. As we started down the steps, an entourage was coming up. In the group was Kennedy. Someone introduced us to the senator, and we said hello. As we walked down the rest of the stairs, I turned to Fritzie and asked, "What do you think?"

She replied, "He needs a haircut!"

The Democratic convention had been held in late March or April. Sometime later, I asked Burdick, "Are you going to get out and campaign?" He and his colleague, Ralph Dewing, were on the Nonpartisan League ticket in the primary; Hocking and Morrison were on the Democratic ticket. Burdick said, "The people in North Dakota know me. If I can't get a win in the primary election without campaigning, I'm not going to get elected this fall."

After Burdick entered the race for Congress, the local Cass County Democratic party held an organizational meeting. At that time, Herschel Lashkowitz, the mayor of Fargo, was making noises like he wanted to be county chairman. Several prominent Democrats came to me and asked if I would consider taking over the party chairmanship. I talked it over with my law partners, Mart and Philip Vogel. Mart gave me the okay and I put my name into the hat. At the county organizational meeting, I was elected and therein lay the tale of a lot of work.

Meanwhile, in the summer of 1958, Burdick and I engaged in a lawsuit as combatants in the district court in Lisbon, North Dakota. I represented a plaintiff, Lyle Pundt, whose hand had been severed in a combine accident. Pundt, seventeen years old, was working on a farm around Lisbon when he got his right arm entangled in the belts of a combine. I brought the lawsuit against the farmer, William Heuther.

Burdick represented Heuther, who was insured by the Farmers Union Insurance Company. During the interrogation of the jury, I asked if they knew Quentin Burdick, and if they knew he was active as the attorney for the Farmers Union. Burdick got so mad about that he would not talk to me for the three days of the lawsuit.

Finally, it became time to go home. Keep in mind, at this time I was, in effect, the manager of Quentin's campaign. I was afraid to ask him for a ride back to Fargo after the lawsuit had been completed, and so I called Fritzie to come and pick me up. I told her of our differences of viewpoint, and she said, "You better make up with Quentin."

So I swallowed my pride and went over to Burdick and asked, "Quentin, can I get a ride back to Fargo with you?"

He said, "Sure." We got in the car, started toward Fargo; he took one look at me and said, "Don't you ever mention Farmers Union to me in another lawsuit."

I won the lawsuit, but got a very small verdict of about $16,500 on a case that I thought was worth $60,000. The Farmers Union appealed the case to the North Dakota Supreme Court, but was turned down. Burdick didn't handle the appeal.

We didn't have a lot of money to finance the general election campaign. Burdick spent a total of $3,500, of which I had raised about $2,500 among my friends and associates in Fargo. In preparation for the fall campaign, I did surveys to find out where the Democrats lived in Fargo so we could call them on Election Day to ensure they would vote. We worked hard, and that paid off in the general election. We had built a good organization of Democrats and Nonpartisan League people in Cass County and they were solidly behind Burdick.

While television did not play a very big role in the campaign, Usher Burdick, Quentin's father and a former congressman, did cut some TV commercials for Quentin. We didn't have much money for television ads, but we did produce one television event that I put together.

On the evening before the November election, we aired a program that included a number of local folks. These people were ordinary citizens — some professionals, some farmers, a housewife and so forth — and the theme of the program was: "What kind of a congressman will Quentin Burdick make?" The answer, of course, was a great congressman.

On Election Day, the job of the party workers was to get out the Democratic vote. Headquarters called every Democratic voter and offered rides, if needed, to the polls and asked the person called to please vote. We did no electioneering as such. Fritzie served as head person in our headquarters. She worked very hard, so hard that her back gave out. We had to put her in the hospital the day after the election.

By holding the county Republican vote to around two thousand or less difference, and with the vote in the west, Burdick could and did win. For the first time in the history of North Dakota, the Democrats had elected a congressman — Quentin Burdick.

The morning after the election, I am in St. John's Hospital with Fritzie, who, even with her bad back, was gloating a bit over the victory.

There's a knock at the door. "Come in," I yelled.

In walks Burdick carrying a big bouquet of roses — maybe a dozen, maybe two.

He was very appreciative. He said, "Fritzie and Myron, without you I could not have made it."

I know we helped, but so did scores and scores of others. It felt good, though, to hear those words.

Sometime later, Congressman Burdick sent us a signed photo of himself with a similar statement: "Without you it would not have happened."

Fritzie and I felt really good about the result. We were proud of Burdick and believed he would be a great congressman.

Burdick and I used to gather in our family room in our home at 225 19th Avenue North and bring out a "pinch" bottle of Scotch whiskey. We'd down it while talking about the campaign. This was always an important meeting to discuss strategy.

Burdick and I continued a very close association after the election. He would call me frequently about bills, particularly controversial ones. The Landrum/Griffin legislation was up before the House. This was anti-labor, but the anti-labor sentiment was strong in the country. Burdick asked me how I thought he should vote. I said to him, "Quentin, do what you think is right, like you always do."

The bill went through, but what Burdick's vote against it did was to ensure that in every election thereafter, he would have unqualified support of the unions, both financial and moral, as well as workers for the campaign.

I visited Burdick in Washington during this time. I remember he kept linen sheets in his office and often slept in his office overnight.

In the next chapter, I will discuss the great Senate campaign of 1960.

— CHAPTER 13 —

What to Do After the Election

So what does a part-time politician such as the chairman of the Democratic Party in Cass County do after the 1958 election? Prepare for the next one! Burdick had been elected to Congress. I did get a kick out of hearing a story circulating among some of my Republican friends, "that Myron Bright is the most dangerous Democratic politician around."

My life would now put renewed focus on my job and family. But in our spare time, Fritzie and I talked politics with an eye toward the 1960 elections, state and federal. The party had elected about forty of its members to the North Dakota Legislature. Now we needed to find someone to run for governor. Fritzie and I and our friends discussed potential candidates.

Not much went on politically in the late fall of 1958, but actively it started up in 1959. Some Nonpartisan League people were beginning to get unhappy about Democrats holding top positions in the newly merged Democratic-NPL Party.

How to keep the party together? I met often to talk politics with my friends, including to Bill Lanier Jr.; John Hove, an English professor at North Dakota State University; Curtis Olson, retail merchant in Fargo; Bernard Majors, an insurance salesman; and others. We often gathered for lunch at Connie Ginakes' restaurant in the downtown area of Fargo. Burdick and I spoke frequently on the telephone.

We addressed the grumbles from some in the NPL wing of the party, and came up with the idea of a fall festival for all to be held in Fargo. This program took a great amount of planning and proved to be a huge success and raised a nice pot of money for the party.

September 20, 1959, the day of the event we called a Jamboree, started out dark, cloudy and a bit rainy. We had purchased hundreds of hamburger patties, together with many bags of potato chips. At 10 o'clock with the bad weather, Fritzie and I thought "disaster." My friend Frank Knox, who was in charge of making and selling hamburgers, asked, "What in the hell can we do with all this meat and buns?"

At about 10:15 a.m., a car came up to the fairgrounds. A lady, her husband and about five children found us at the refreshment stand. She said, "We just came in from Bottineau, North Dakota. Where do I get free coffee?" This visit served as a harbinger of a great day for the Democrats. Hubert Humphrey arrived by commercial aircraft and we laid out a red carpet for him. As he stepped out of the airplane, the sun emerged from the clouds.

At least twenty-five hundred people attended the program. Humphrey, Burdick and the forty Democratic state legislators occupied a platform. Everyone had a fine time. John D. Paulson, editor of *The Forum*, Fargo's daily newspaper, said, "I never saw as many Democrats in one place before."

Former President Harry Truman addressed a Democratic rally in Minot that fall of 1959, which also was a huge success, also attended by about twenty-five hundred people. Fritzie, her friend Helen Pepple, another woman friend and I had the great pleasure of a short visit with Truman in his hotel room. When we entered the room, the former president was seated on a couch, in front of him a bottle of Black and White scotch on a low coffee table. Truman looked as neat as a pin.

I talked to the former president about North Dakota politics and mentioned Congressman Quentin Burdick. Truman picked up on it and said, "I love Western United States history, and Usher Burdick, father of Quentin, has the best collection of Western history books. I'd love to get my hands on them."

I told Truman about our money-raising plan where we gave each precinct committee person round cartons, the size of a roll of dimes. Each carton would hold a hundred coins. The committee people would pass out cartons to friends and hope the cartons would come back filled with dimes.

After a short conversation, we said goodbye and left. This occasion was the first time in her political days that Fritzie never opened her mouth.

On returning to our room, I just joyfully bounced up and down on the bed.

Truman made a great speech that evening before a packed school gymnasium. I'll never forget this line from his talk as he pounded the podium saying these words, "They have coined a new term 'agribusiness.' You know what that means—they are going to give the farmers the business." Wild applause with yells came from the audience.

The year ended with the death of North Dakota's long-time Senator William Langer at the age of seventy-three on Nov. 7, 1959. My claim to fame about the Langer funeral is that Senator Estes Kefauver of Tennessee borrowed and wore my zippered overshoes to keep his feet warm.

This begins another chapter in my political life.

— CHAPTER 14 —

Quentin Runs for Senate, Guy for Governor, JFK for President

During the Christmas holiday season of 1959, Burdick and I spoke about the Senate vacancy caused by Langer's death. "Quentin," I said, "stay where you are. You can be a congressman like Usher, your dad, for many years."

Burdick replied, "This is my chance and I'm going for it."

The die was cast. Burdick would run for the Senate to replace the late "Wild Bill" Langer.

At an Elks Club Saturday night dance in Fargo during that same Christmas holiday season, I danced with Jocelyn Birch Peterson. With some shyness in her voice, she said, "Myron, I had a date with Quentin." I kidded her a bit, not thinking that a serious relationship was in the wind. Little did I know. The next winter, 1960, he and I were sitting around in my north Fargo family home drinking from a pinch bottle of great scotch and talking politics. In the middle of a conversation, Burdick said, "Myron, I'm engaged to Jocie. I've given her a diamond ring."

I straightened up from my tipped chair and uttered these words: "My God, that's a disaster. You'll lose all the women's sympathy vote because you are now a widower. Tell Jocie to wear the ring around her neck, not on her finger!"

I added to Burdick that Jocie, a Republican, would be an albatross around his neck and the worst handicap he could have for the election.

Wouldn't you know it, Quentin turned right around a day later and told Jocie my story. She wasn't happy about my comments and displayed the ring on her finger.

As it proved out, Jocie was not his big handicap, but rather she was a real asset. Who knows, maybe it was the votes of her college sorority sisters, Gamma Phi Beta, that helped Burdick win in a very close election.

I've had many laughs about these comments with Jocie and Quentin, and Jocie keeps reminding me of my big mistake. Fortunately, in those days, the press was not alerted to the engagement. I doubt that many people in the state knew.

Although we were particularly interested in the Senate race, that contest was only part of the great political brew of 1960. In that year, three political offices occupied my mind and my actions:
1. The Democratic presidential primary and the national election race between JFK, Democrat, and Richard Nixon, Republican
2. The race for the U.S. Senate from North Dakota, Quentin N. Burdick, Democrat, versus John W. Davis, a Republican and the incumbent governor
3. The race for governor among William (Bill) Guy, Democrat; C.P. Dahl, a Republican; and Herschel Lashkowitz, an independent.

So, let's start from the beginning, January 1, 1960, and talk about our activities during that fateful, fulfilling and crucial political year. But before I do, I want to make clear: When I say *I*, the word means *we*. My wife and I acted as partners in the political years; our decisions were mutual. Fritzie possessed a natural flair for politics. She seemed to sense what was right. She also served as a hostess and greeter. To the extent I served successfully as adviser to political candidates or otherwise engaged in party politics with success, I give Fritzie equal credit.

Politics, politics, politics. That subject occupied our busy minds. As a Democrat, I knew who would run for Senate — Quentin Burdick. But who could we put up for governor? We knew early in the year that Republican Governor John Davis would run for the Senate, and his term as governor would end.

Sometime in January, close friends Eli Dobervich and his wife, June, invited Fritzie, me, and Bill and Jean Guy to dinner at the Dobervich home in Fargo. Eli and I were "Rangers" in the sense that we had grown up on the Minnesota Iron Range. We both were WWII veterans and I served as the lawyer for his corporation that manufactured fruit jams. His wife, June, came from an old Moorhead family — Probstfield. She taught school.

Guy, a Navy veteran of WWII, farmed near Amenia. A Democratic stalwart, he was elected to the state House of Representatives in 1958. His wife, Jean, graduated with him from North Dakota Agricultural College (now North Dakota State University). She was a homemaker and a beautiful, accomplished woman.

At the dinner and afterwards, the drinks flowed freely. Following the meal, we talked about a favorite subject to us all — politics, particularly who could the party draft to run for governor.

During our animated conversations, Eli fell asleep on the floor. He had consumed a few drinks of liquor. In the middle of our discussion, Eli rose from his stupor, raised his arm and exclaimed "Guy for governor!"

The conversation stopped.

"That's a laugh," commented Bill. Jean said nothing.

Fritzie and I echoed, "Great idea!"

Thus the idea of Guy for governor began percolating from the Brights to others in the party.

The scene now shifts to early February 1960. Jack Kennedy came to Jamestown to make a political speech at a dinner sponsored by the Democratic Party. About that time, the Democratic nominations for the presidential race had begun to heat up. Announced contenders included Kennedy, Senator Lyndon Baines Johnson from Texas, Senator Hubert Humphrey of Minnesota, Senator Stuart Symington of Missouri, and former Illinois governor and prior Democratic presidential candidate Adlai Stevenson. I was a lukewarm Stevenson supporter with Humphrey close behind. My Irish friend, John Murphy of Fargo, kept urging me to support Kennedy. Thus I thought it important to meet JFK personally, so I made arrangements to attend the Kennedy speech at Jamestown.

I also was thinking about the coming Senate election and Burdick's campaign, and pondering which candidate for president on the Democratic ticket could most help Burdick.

Bill and Jean Guy drove to Jamestown in their station wagon. Bill Lanier, the state Democratic Party chairman, and I rode along. En route, I said to the Guys, "How about Bill Guy for governor?" In the front seat, Bill and Jean did not say yes or no. That was good enough — they didn't say no. That meant OK. The ride became an early kickoff of "Guy for Governor."

After listening to the Kennedy speech in the ballroom of the Gladstone Hotel, I was convinced. Kennedy was my man for president.

Following the banquet, the Democrats who attended met in a large room of the hotel. I took it upon myself to call Kennedy. Here's the unusual telephone conversation and my reaction:

Myron: (A person answers) I want to talk to Senator Kennedy.

Voice: This is Jack Kennedy.

Myron: (Thinking the voice must be some aide to the Senator) I want to talk to Senator Kennedy.

Voice: I am Senator Kennedy.

I was bowled over, thinking an important person like JFK would have an aide or someone like that to take his calls.

I finally realized that I was talking to "The Senator."

I explained who I was, Democratic Party chairman of the largest county in North Dakota and close friend to Congressman Burdick. I asked for a personal visit. Kennedy said he would join the meeting in a few minutes and there we could visit.

We talked when he came to the meeting room. I don't remember the conversation but it was friendly. I found him just down to earth. I do have some correspondence from that visit. Kennedy wrote the following:

> February 16, 1960
>
> Dear Myron:
>
> I certainly enjoyed seeing you during my recent visit to North Dakota and I appreciate your friendly interest in my presidential race.
>
> It was indeed good of you to invite me to appear in Fargo [in June of 1960]. At the moment it is difficult to see what my schedule will be in June, but I will see what can be worked out. If you could give me the details of what you have in mind, I will give it every consideration.
>
> With every good wish, I am
>
> Sincerely,
> John F. Kennedy

I sent a copy of the letter to Burdick stating, "Quentin, the date of our special election is the 28th of June. Will you call Senator Kennedy and explain?"

He responded, "What are you talking about?"

At that early date, I smelled that in the coming campaign for U.S. senator from North Dakota, Republicans would certainly mount a smear campaign asserting that Burdick had ties to Communists. Such smears were made against Burdick in his successful race for Congress in 1958 and in his earlier challenge against then-Senator Milton Young in 1956. In essence, the smear asserted that Burdick was soft on Communism, charging that he was something of a "pinko." In the earlier days, these smear artists had said, among other things, that Burdick may not be a Communist, but he is close to it because he served on the platform committee of the Henry Wallace Progressive [alleged to be Communist-tainted] Party of 1956. We needed to defeat or defuse such a charge in the coming election.

I strongly believed that to kill a smear, positive action must be taken. Mere denials like, "No, I'm not a pinko" seldom proved effective. What better way could there be to block any such smear by having the number one anti-Communist senator, John F. Kennedy, a Catholic, put his arm around Burdick and say in effect, "Congressman Burdick is a great American."

As a result of my meeting in February of 1960 with Kennedy, he agreed to come to Fargo in June to support Burdick, provided that only he, and no other Democratic candidate, would speak at whatever affair would be planned.

This arrangement led to Senator Burdick's great big birthday party on Sunday, June 19, 1960, in Fargo, only nine days before the special Senate election. Burdick celebrated his 52nd birthday that day, which also was Father's Day.

But let's return to early 1960 and relate the general political activity. The plan to nominate Guy for governor was in full gear.

The Cass County delegates to the state's joint Democratic Party and Nonpartisan League convention, scheduled in April of 1960, strongly supported Guy. But getting him the state party endorsement was no pushover. Bill and his father had been members of the North Dakota Farm Bureau, a conservative organization whose members generally supported Republicans for public office.

The other large farm organization, the Farmers Union, was liberal. Its members strongly supported the Democratic-NPL Party. Farmers Union members who were delegates to the convention didn't easily cotton to Guy.

At the convention, when the Guy opponents went to Burdick seeking to oppose Guy, Burdick said in effect, "Who have you got as a candidate?" The answer was "nobody special." Burdick strongly supported Guy and the opposition crumbled. Guy also satisfied the Farmers Union members with his liberal views on government — whatever "liberal" meant.

Guy received the endorsement, and Charles Tighe, a Bismarck lawyer, was endorsed for lieutenant governor.

The Democratic Party convention unanimously endorsed Burdick for Senate. The stage became set for one of the most important elections in North Dakota history.

— CHAPTER 15 —

Birthday Bash with JFK Boosts Burdick

As we approached the 1960 campaign, Bill Lanier, the state Democratic chairman, announced that the party didn't need any outside help in the campaign. However, Burdick's opponent, John Davis, got plenty of outside assistance. Nelson Rockefeller, who was running for the Republican presidential endorsement, came to Fargo during the campaign, as did several other dignitaries, including Vice President Richard Nixon.

Fritzie and I, and the two Murphys (John and Rosemary) got our heads together. We recognized it would be great for public relations and a wonderful campaign affair to have a birthday party for Burdick on June 19, 1960. But we didn't want the Democratic Party to put on the celebration. Rather, Burdick's son, Jon, and three daughters, Jan, Jennifer and Jessica, would sponsor the event. (All the children's names began with "J," probably from Marietta Janecky, their mother).

As I had mentioned, JFK had tentatively agreed to come to Fargo to help Burdick. Jan Burdick, Quentin's oldest child, issued this news release which stated:

> NEWS RELEASE FROM JAN BURDICK
>
> June 11, 1960
>
> The family of Congressman Quentin Burdick announces further plans for their dad's birthday party to be held Sunday, June 19th, at the Red River Valley Fairgrounds in Fargo. In

case of rain the gathering will be held at the Fargo Civic Memorial Auditorium. The time of the party will be 2:30 p.m. (Daylight Time) or 1:30 p.m. (Standard Time).

Mr. Manny Marget, well-known radio personality in the Fargo-Moorhead area and station manager of KVOX will serve as master of ceremonies for the party. Members of the Burdick family who will attend are former Congressman Usher L. Burdick of Williston; Judge and Mrs. Eugene Burdick, also of Williston; Congressman and Mrs. Robert Levering of Fredrickstown, Ohio (relatives of the Burdicks); and Dr. and Mrs. J.W. Janecky of Barnesville, Minnesota (Mrs. Burdick's parents).

Senator John Kennedy of Massachusetts has accepted an invitation to be one of the honored guests of the family. An invitation has also been sent to Mrs. Eleanor Roosevelt, wife of the late President Franklin D. Roosevelt. Her reply is expected within the next couple of days.

Jan Burdick spoke Friday, June 10th, to a meeting in Grand Forks and extended the birthday invitation to all the residents in the Grand Forks area. She attended a rally being held in Barney, North Dakota, Saturday, June 11th, and invited all the friends and workers.

Spot radio announcements ran on June 17th and 18th. A bulk rate mailing of an invitation on a postcard went to every household in Fargo and West Fargo. The text of the handwritten postcard read:

Dear Friends,

You are cordially invited to a "Birthday Party" for our father, Rep. Quentin N. Burdick, Father's Day—June 19—Red River Valley Fair Grounds—2:30 p.m. daylight time—(1:30 standard time)—Fargo, North Dakota

We have invited as our special guests, Sen. John Kennedy and his wife. And also many relatives including our grandfather, Usher L. Burdick, who will all help us celebrate Dad's birthday.

> Bring your family and enjoy an afternoon of entertainment, ice cream and fun!
>
> Hope you can come!
>
> > The Burdick children
> > Jessica, Jennifer, Jan Mary, and Jon

Additionally, a flier was distributed with the pictures of Burdick and JFK.

Preliminary to the birthday party, of course, we got every facility in Fargo nailed down. That included the Fairgrounds, where we intended to have the celebration, and the Civic Center, where we would have a Democratic Party gathering or hold the party itself if it rained. We also reserved all of the public park facilities — that is, picnic facilities in town. This became important because Vice President Nixon also came to town on June 19 and there wasn't any place for him to hold an event. His political appearance had to be continued over until the following day, Monday.

We had a man from the Farmers Union in Jamestown living with the Brights for several weeks and working with us in the planning and arrangements for this birthday party. He arranged to obtain a train carrying open freight cars behind the engine. The train ran on wheels rather than on tracks. All of the dignitaries rode on the little train from the airport to the birthday party. A picture of that scene with Burdick, Kennedy, Burdick's daughter, Jenny, and Senator Stuart Symington appeared in every major paper in the country the following day, June 20. The photo and the birthday party also was a lead article in *Life* magazine during the week after the Burdick birthday party.

There are so many stories about this event. First of all, the candidates for the Democratic nomination for president (and they included Kennedy, Lyndon Johnson, Hubert Humphrey and Symington) wanted to come. Because Burdick had promised Kennedy he would be the sole speaker, JFK was the only candidate who came at Burdick's invitation. However, LBJ sent a representative, the new governor of Hawaii, John Burns. Symington came personally. He had talked to the Democratic national committeewoman, Daphne Nygard of Jamestown, who said he could participate and so he did.

An amusing, maybe hilarious, planning conversation with a member of Kennedy's entourage occurred on a Saturday about two weeks before Burdick's birthday. The Murphys and Brights had been visiting that evening at the Bright home. What were we discussing? Obviously the planned Burdick birthday party.

Some of the arrangements about the JFK visit to Fargo remained unsettled. On that Saturday evening, we knew that Kennedy had carried his campaign to Minnesota. As I recall, a campaign event occurred at one of the large Minneapolis hotels, probably the Nicollet Hotel. The four of us — Fritzie, Myron, John and Rosemary — agreed that we should try to talk to Kennedy or one of his assistants about the program for our party. So I made a person-to-person call to Minneapolis to my friend and former law school classmate, Orville Freeman, then the governor of Minnesota. I figured Freeman could act as a connector between the Fargo planners (Murphys, Brights) and JFK. After a long wait on the phone, Freeman's aide and press secretary answered.

After explaining our purpose, that of making some final arrangements for the forthcoming birthday party, the aide said, "Hold on. I'll see what I can do?" Following a considerable wait, maybe fifteen minutes, a mellow voice sounded on the telephone. The voice said, "This is Sargent Shriver. What can I help you with?"

In my mind, I envisioned some Army sergeant who I thought was a lower-level assistant to JFK. But I would pass on my problems and requests. My conversations were something like the following with my addressing the man as "sergeant." I said, among other things:

"Sergeant, find out what time Kennedy can come to Fargo."

"Sergeant, will Kennedy appear with Quentin at a press conference?" and on and on, sergeant, this and sergeant that.

I soon learned that "Sargent" was not "sergeant."

When the telephone conversation ended, John Murphy asked, "Mike, who were you talking to?"

I answered, "Oh, some Army sergeant with Kennedy."

John Murphy responded, "Hey, you were talking to Sargent Shriver, JFK's brother-in-law, and the guy who runs the Merchandise Mart in Chicago."

I thought, wow! What a mistake!

But through the conference call, we had arranged a preliminary schedule of events relating to JFK's presence at the birthday party.

(Adding an aside, Shriver and I later met face to face, in the summer of 1972, at a hotel in Rapid City, South Dakota. Shriver then was a vice presidential candidate on the ticket with Senator George McGovern. I was at a judicial meeting of federal judges. When we met, both of us recalled that telephone conversation in June of 1960 and we laughed about it.)

Fritzie had been in touch with Kennedy's brother-in-law, Steve Smith, for weeks before our event. He would call her Mrs. Myron, and he said, "You arrange this dinner for Jack, but don't do it under the Kennedy name because if you do it that way, the price will go up double."

So Fritzie arranged with Inga, the banquet arranger of the Gardner Hotel, to put this dinner on for Kennedy and for all the North Dakota delegates to the national Democratic Party convention that would nominate candidates for president and vice president. Fritzie had been informed by Smith that Kennedy liked to have two bottles of Heineken beer with his dinner, that he would eat dinner in the hotel and that he would meet with the delegates later.

"Mrs. Bright," Inga said, "I can't do that. We don't serve beer on Sunday."

And Fritzie replied, "Listen, Inga. On Saturday, go and buy two bottles of beer, put them in the refrigerator and then on Sunday you can put the beer in Senator Kennedy's room."

Actually, the way it worked out was that Kennedy came in around noon, prior to the program. Symington had arrived at 9 a.m. The birthday celebration was in the early afternoon. And then later we had a Democratic Party gathering. Kennedy met with the delegates to the Democratic National Convention at a dinner.

Wallace Lindell, a close friend who also was an assistant editor at *The Forum* newspaper, refused to publish some of our news releases about the event, saying something to the effect, "We're not kids. We know the Democratic Party is behind this affair. Don't have these Burdick kids give us news stories."

So we thought we'd fix him. We did get a communication from Eleanor Roosevelt indicating that she might come to the event so we released this information to the television news media, but not *The Forum*. The TV stations all ran the release as main stories. Eleanor didn't appear, but that's beside the point. Lindell called Fritzie and asked, "How come I didn't get the story?" Fritzie responded, "Listen, Wally. You said you weren't going to run any stories and that you weren't going to be taken in by these kids, so you didn't get the story." From then on the attitude of The Forum was better.

I had written a letter addressed to Symington, who was scheduled to have a press conference on the morning of June 19th with Burdick. In my letter, I outlined the issues in the campaign for the Senate and the importance of Burdick getting elected, and gave Symington some tips for the news conference. I put Bill Lanier in charge of Symington and gave him my letter to the Missouri senator. Unfortunately, Lanier didn't show up and therefore Symington didn't get the letter.

The Symington-Burdick press conference proved to be a real disaster. The press asked questions of Symington but he never included Quentin in his answers; Quentin sat like a bump on a log all morning. It was not a very auspicious start.

When Kennedy flew into town, we had the Shriners' motorcycle patrol escort him to the Fairgrounds in advance of the "train." He, Jenny Burdick, Symington and Quentin all rode the train from the airport into the Fairgrounds, where we held the birthday party. It was a most successful event, with the theme: "This is Your Life, Quentin Burdick."

A piano was to be delivered at the Fairgrounds. John Murphy and I were trying to coordinate arrangements so everything would be set, but by 12:30 p.m., no piano appeared. The program was scheduled for about 1:30 and we were getting worried. Fritzie and I had a lovely piano in our little house on the north side of Fargo and, while at the Fairgrounds, I saw and stopped a Thompson Movers' truck. I asked the driver to deliver my piano. The driver had me call his employer. Bill Thompson, the president of Thompson Movers, was a friend of Burdick's, and he gave permission for the truck to haul our piano.

Fritzie wasn't home when we started to load our piano into the truck. When Fritzie arrived on the scene and saw what was going on, she started to cry, "Oh, my beautiful piano; you're going to ruin my piano."

In the meantime, the arranged-for piano did get delivered to the Fairgrounds, and we moved ours back in our house. All was well.

While I've mentioned the Murphys and Brights in the planning of the affair, I would be amiss in not noting that the Cass County Democratic-NPL Party members participated with enthusiasm. Joe Poer, a Teamsters truck driver and my special assistant, and Margaret Waxler, in charge of campaign headquarters, gave great assistance. My friend and fellow Fargo lawyer, Frank Knox, handled crowd arrangements with excellent results. Here's an outline of the proposed program:

BURDICK BIRTHDAY PARTY

10:35 A.M.	HECTOR AIRPORT, FARGO — Cong. Quentin Burdick and family will meet Senator Stuart Symington of Missouri, arriving Northwest Airlines.
10:45 A.M.	NEWS CONFERENCE — Hector Airport — Cong. Burdick and Sen. Symington. All press, TV & Radio personnel invited.
11:15 A.M.	Cong. Burdick and Sen. Symington will visit Veterans Hospital, Fargo.
12:00 Noon	Lunch
1:00 P.M.	Gates open at Fairgrounds, Casselton Band will play.
2:00 P.M.	Jenny Burdick, on behalf of family, will meet Senator Kennedy's plane, arriving North Ramp of Airport. Sen. Kennedy will be accompanied by: Hugh Sidey — *Time* magazine; Chalmers Roberts — *Washington Post*; Charles Von Freund — CBS; Joe Alsop — Syndicated Columnist; Douglas Cornell — Associated Press; Adalbert (Ziggy) de Segonzac — France *Soi*
	Charles Roach — News Representative
	Kenneth O'Donnell — Staff
	Jenny Burdick, Quentin Burdick, Sen. Symington and Sen. Kennedy will ride the BURDICK BIRTHDAY EXPRESS (Furnished by Jamestown Railroad men), Engine & Cars to the Fairgrounds.
2:15-4:00 P.M.	Birthday Party
4:00-4:30 P.M.	Participants stop for refreshments at home of Dr. G. Wilson Hunter, 11th Avenue & Broadway, Fargo.

4:45-5:15 P.M.	Fargo Civic Memorial Auditorium — Open press conference Sen. Kennedy and Cong. Burdick.
5:15-6:15 P.M.	Informal party for visitors, guests, party workers.
6:15-7:00 P.M.	Sen. Kennedy, rest and supper, Gardner Hotel.
7:00-7:30 P.M.	Sen. Kennedy meets with North Dakota delegates to national convention.
7:45 P.M.	Depart to Hector Airport, Fargo.

This was a birthday party. Right! My close friend, Paul Feder, operated the Brownee's Bakery in Fargo, which provided a birthday cake of immense proportions. His chief baker, Frank Lang, baked the cake, and it was a beauty, standing about four feet in height with several layers.

The cake, incidentally, played a role in Burdick's election. Native Americans from North Dakota reservations came to the party in several vehicles and they entertained the crowd with their traditional dances. Later, Fritzie sent part of the cake with them and said, "Bring it out to the reservation," with further admonition that the Native Americans get out the vote for Quentin. They did, overwhelmingly. Without the Native Americans' vote, Burdick wouldn't have won the election.

According to the tally of free ice cream that we gave out to the attendees, there were about six thousand people at the party. Never in history had there been a crowd like that at a political gathering in North Dakota.

Fritzie had been hard at work during the birthday party. Finally, I did introduce her to Kennedy. She grinned from ear to ear. He had her vote and her political love, too.

I had listened to JFK speak at the Fairgrounds with newspaper man Hugh Sidey of *Time* magazine. Sidey kept saying, "He's got it, he's going to be nominated."

The speech drew thundering applause. Kennedy made his speaking points by pounding his right fist into his left hand. He gave a warm and complimentary endorsement of Burdick for the U.S. Senate. I have two mementos from Kennedy of that wonderful day. A photograph taken of JFK at the Hunter home hangs on my office wall. The photo bears the inscription: "To Myron Bright with warm regards, John F. Kennedy." Even though the writing has faded some, those words are embedded in a warm memory. JFK also gave me a signed copy of his book, *Profiles in Courage.*

How lucky for me!

After the celebration, we all went to Dr. Hunter's house on north Broadway for a little refreshment. While at the Hunter house, Burdick announced that he wasn't going to appear on the scheduled press conference at 5:00 p.m. He explained that he didn't want to sit like a lump on a log. I think Symington had left by this time.

John Murphy called Kennedy over: "Jack, Jack, come on over here. Senator Burdick doesn't want to go to the press conference. He thinks nobody will ask him a question."

Kennedy came by and responded, "Listen, Quentin, you go to that press conference. I'll take care of you." And he did.

During the afternoon session at the Fargo Civic Memorial Auditorium, national and local press reporters gathered with Kennedy and Burdick.

Burdick and Kennedy faced the media. But the reporters again questioned only Kennedy. Was another press fiasco in the making?

After initial questions, the agriculture issue surfaced. A reporter asked Kennedy, "What can be done to raise farm prices?"

Kennedy gave a short response to the question, and then said this: "Congressman Burdick knows a lot more about farmers' problems than I do." He turned to Burdick. "Congressman Burdick," he said, "what do you think can be done to raise farm prices?"

My friend Senator Burdick rose to the occasion with a fine statement. The press conference continued with equal participation of both JFK and Burdick.

That incident in political history was captured by *Life* magazine in a photograph taken at that press conference. The photographer snapped his lens from the side, and the picture shows the back of Burdick's head with the elbow outstretched, but his hand on his forehead. Etched within the triangle made by the crook of his arm is the handsome face of Kennedy. A print of that picture hangs prominently in my chambers in Fargo. I often look at it and recall the Kennedy principle: "Share the spotlight with others." I have often reflected on that philosophy and have tried to follow it. It has served me well.

Kennedy left on Sunday evening, just as Nixon arrived. We had a large traffic jam near the airport. About ten days later, the people of North Dakota elected a new senator. By about one-half vote per precinct, or about eleven hundred votes, Burdick defeated his opponent and entered the Senate, where he served for thirty-two years. Fargo politics was a lead story in newspapers nationwide.

The reason the birthday party was so important, in my opinion, is that it gave Burdick wide exposure to the people of the state. TV Channel 4, operated and owned by John Boler, videotaped the whole program and ran it the following Sunday, two days before the election. That was bound to have drawn sufficient voters to turn the election around because Quentin only won by a very small margin. It was probably the most successful political affair I have had anything to do with. The Nixon appearance on behalf of John Davis was anti-climactic.

Senator Burdick wrote Fritzie and me the following letter on the one-year anniversary of the birthday party:

> June 19, 1961
>
> Dear Fritzie and Mike,
>
> Celebrities on hand . . . . . train repaired . . . . .
> Indians on time for cash . . . . . press converted . . . . .
> walk when car doesn't run . . . . . ice cream plentiful
> . . . . . but Nixon unavailable 1964 . . . . . Many thanks
> for that memorable day!
>
> Best regards,
>
> Quentin N. Burdick

— CHAPTER 16 —

Vignettes

Here are some additional vignettes on the 1960 campaign:

At the Democratic Party convention in the spring, prior to the June special election, Fritzie and Mae Burdick, the wife of Quentin Burdick's brother Eugene, got together to work up a campaign song for Quentin. Initially, the song was put to the tune of "My Darling Clementine," but later it was sung to the tune of "Slattery's Irish March" at the suggestion of John Murphy. This song was played and sung by the enthusiastic Democratic attendees at all of the party rallies. It was the subject of a tune by Stuart Symington's son Jimmy, who came to the Burdick birthday party, sang the song and cut a record of it. The song was televised as the TV cameras covered the rally.

As I remember it, the song went something like this:

"B" for Burdick "B" for Burdick
Let's support him every one.
He's the champion of the people
and the man we've chosen to run.
We elected him and we'll elect him
and our senator he will be.
"B" for Burdick "B" for Burdick
For a smashing victory!
Oh the NPL and Democrats are going all the way
to put good ol' Quentin in the senate of the USA.
We respect him and we'll elect him

and our senator he will be.
"B" for Burdick "B" for Burdick
For a smashing victory!

The 1960 campaign was interesting and tough. Republicans endorsed Davis, a handsome, very nice man, and a guy big in the American Legion circle, to run for the vacant Senate seat.

Mercer Cross, staff writer for the *Minneapolis Tribune,* wrote a story on June 13, 1960, with the headline "Burdick Faces Smear Tactics in North Dakota Campaign." Here are some excerpts:

> A printed sheet titled "Quentin Burdick and his Communist Associates" is being distributed in North Dakota ...
>
> Burdick, the state's first Democratic congressman, is running for the senate in a special election June 28 ...
>
> The printed material being circulated anonymously this year takes at least two forms, a 4½-page statement and a two-page condensed version ...
>
> The statements cite Burdick's membership on the platform committee of Henry Wallace's Progressive party in that year ... He is not a Communist or pro-Communist, but his political thinking has often gotten him in questionable company ...
>
> The anti-Burdick material is unsigned and sent in plain envelopes. It has been mailed from several places, including Minot, North Dakota, Jamestown, North Dakota, Aberdeen, South Dakota, and Sioux Falls, South Dakota ...
>
> Burdick blames Republican "pros" for the attacks. The Republicans deny knowing anything about this ...
>
> "This election may determine [whether smears work] on a nationwide basis," Burdick said, "Because they brought the four top Republican pros into North Dakota."
>
> The four pros he spoke of are Victor A. Johnston, Washington, director of the Republican senatorial campaign committee; his assistant, John Underhill; Edward Terrell, Madison, Wis., director of the GOP national committee, and John F. Milles, Milwaukee, Wis., a field man for the Republican congressional campaign committee ...

> The governor (Davis) added, "Mr. Burdick should make it clear why he was associated with an organization dominated by such a Communist influence at that time. I feel the people should know Mr. Burdick's record."

Incidentally, on June 16, 1960, Lawrence Knutson, editor of the *Kindred Tribune,* a country weekly, printed a piece that was later sent to all news media. His title was "My Two Cents Worth." Here's an excerpt:

> Now it has been reported that a Mr. Johnston and Mr. Mills, two outsiders, are directing the Davis for Senate drive in North Dakota. I reported portions of a *Milwaukee Journal* article on another page of this paper I think should interest all Republicans and Democrats in North Dakota.
>
> I say vote for Davis if you believe he is the man to serve the people of North Dakota or vote for Burdick if you think he is the man but I cannot subscribe to outsiders telling us how to vote. North Dakota has been here a long time and we've done a fine job to date, and I think we can continue to do a good job without any outside help.
>
> We believe everyone in North Dakota is interested in good government and good representation in Congress regardless of party. We believe you should check into this matter and find out to your own personal satisfaction just what is going on. We called the hotel and we found out that there was a Mr. Victor Johnston and a Mr. Jack Mills registered at the hotel. If these gentlemen have the power reported in the *Milwaukee Journal* article, then our state politics, as well as democracy, is surely in danger.

I had furnished Knutson information contained in letters I had received from national Democratic campaign sources. I take some pride of working with Knutson in preparing the article.

The text of the article above was reproduced in a pamphlet by John Murphy. With the state Democratic-NPL officials, I arranged to have ninety thousand pamphlets printed and delivered to party persons at the birthday party and to Democratic Party officials from almost every county in North Dakota. They then delivered individual copies to people in their counties.

I later heard from some Republican friends who said the pamphlet punctured the picture that Republicans always acted honorably in a political campaign. The article became a powerful anti-smear piece for Burdick.

One question we faced, among others, was how we could get independent voters, soft Republicans and nonvoters in an election, to support Burdick. One effective campaign activity was an organization set up by the women in the party called "Busy Bees for Burdick."

Here is how it worked: A woman active in Democratic politics would invite her friends, regardless of their political views, to her house for coffee and to do some election campaign work. For example, Mrs. Phyllis Hunter, wife of Dr. Hunter, assigned her coffee friends (regardless of political leanings) the task of stuffing and addressing envelopes with Burdick campaign material. At the meeting, the hostess distributed campaign buttons about the size of a nickel. The face of the button showed a bee and the legend "Busy Bees for Burdick."

These individuals worked for Quentin and for the most part became Burdick supporters and voters. The busy bees operated all over in Fargo.

All hail: Busy Bees for Burdick!

One of our critical efforts to elect Burdick was getting out the Democratic vote, so we contacted people who were likely to need absentee ballots because they were shut-ins, sick or physically couldn't go to the polls. Our lists weren't the best. I remember taking a number of ballots for absentee voters and I'd see the people make X's in the left-hand column, the Republican column, even though those people had been listed as Democrats. But nothing is perfect.

On the Saturday before the election, we had a big meeting at our home. Present were a number of the campaign people who worked with me in Fargo, along with Bill Guy, our Democratic candidate for governor, and a fellow by the name of Gray who was a high official with COPE, the political action committee of the labor movement. At that time, Gray revealed the plan for getting out the vote.

The state statutes authorized poll watchers, who would sit next to or with the election officials and check off as they appeared the known Democrats or known labor people who were likely to vote Democratic. Then, at various times during the day, duplicates of those lists would be given to runners who would bring the list to Democratic headquarters. Volunteers would review the list, call those people who had not yet voted, urge them to get to the polls and provide rides.

Although the Senate race between Burdick and Davis was on a separate ballot, this was also a primary election for which the voter had to request either a Republican ballot or a Democratic ballot.

John Murphy came over to me and said, "Myron, you can't let them do that. That's going to be a way for the union to punish those people in the union who don't vote as the union officials want them to." In other words, the possibility existed that a poll watcher would know when a potential Democratic voter was calling for a Republican ballot and would make note of that. Murphy said that this would cause all kinds of problems and we couldn't let them do that.

We discussed the matter and I came to the conclusion that this would be very dangerous. I said the poll watchers would have to be outside the polling site.

This was the first time in the history, as far as I know, that poll watchers had been used in North Dakota. It was a new situation and, if the wrong story got out, it could deter people from voting. I didn't want to take any chances.

I think I made the right decision. The next day in Sunday's newspaper, two days prior to the election, Ken Fitch, the Cass County Republican chairman, made a statement that Democrats would have poll watchers reporting whether union members were voting the Democratic ticket. I responded for the Democratic Party and said in effect, Ken Fitch is full of *fitch*. In other words, there is nothing to it. So, there was no story, no adverse publicity.

Having the poll watchers outside worked out pretty well. Voters were asked their names and their names were checked off. It worked just as though the poll watchers were within the voting area.

Fritzie ran Democratic headquarters, the main floor of the old Fargo National Bank Building at the corner of NP Avenue and Broadway. It was a busy place. On election night, the FBI came along, wanting to see me because some campaign literature had been distributed without listing the sponsor as required by law. Fritzie almost had a heart attack thinking I had done something wrong. Fortunately, I hadn't.

The night before the election, we had a big meeting at the labor temple in Fargo. I made a speech and talked about these two guys who were the smear artists. This really got our people worked up and ready to get out the vote the next day.

I don't remember what I did on election night. Fritzie and I were superstitious of election parties because almost every time we had one in recent years, our candidates lost. I know we were up most of the night listening to the returns. At the time I went to bed, I think Davis was ahead by something like twelve thousand or fourteen thousand votes. We were still hopeful because we felt that Burdick's great strength lay in the western part of the state, where some results were still to be reported.

On Wednesday morning, about 10:30, I went over to Jocelyn Birch's (soon-to-be Mrs. Burdick) home to talk to Quentin and Jocie. Things looked pretty gloomy. I think at that time, Quentin was approximately two thousand votes behind Davis.

I began drafting a concession statement that congratulated Davis on his victory. While working on the statement, we got a call. John Pancrantz, one of our party workers, was following the election returns at election headquarters at *The Forum*. He said, "Hold everything! There's just been found a tabulating mistake at the election headquarters here at *The Forum*. There is a two thousand vote error and Quentin still has a chance."

I tore up the concession statement and went back to my law office.

The margin shrunk to about three hundred votes and then about 1:00 or 2:00 p.m., the margin increased again to about seven hundred votes in favor of Davis. Things again looked pretty sad and dim.

A couple hours later I went home. Some friends were over, but Fritzie and I were both completely exhausted. I had very little sleep the night before, so about 5:00 p.m. we went to bed and I fell asleep. An hour later or thereabouts, the telephone rang. It was Rosemary Murphy. She shrieked, "Quentin just went ahead by fifty votes. The Indian vote has come in!" We shouted with glee.

At that point, we got a call from a reporter of *Time* magazine asking about Quentin Burdick. Fritzie answered the phone and just at that minute she lost her voice and couldn't speak.

I took over the phone and told the reporter about Burdick.

The years from 1960 to 1968 are somewhat of a blur to me. Burdick and I talked often. I was his close confidant and we enjoyed a very good and close friendship.

— CHAPTER 17 —

After the Ball and Burdick Benefit of '64

The election was over. Quentin Burdick had been elected to the United States Senate. I was reminded of that old tune that goes something like this: "After the ball is over, after the game is won," and so on.

My body was tired, my mind was happy and I was looking forward to further political activity as chairman of the Cass County Democratic Party. But life changes and here's the story of my change in perspective.

What did I want out of politics? Was I looking for a job? Was I looking to change my occupation? Was I looking to leave Fargo and for the political arena of national politics? The answer is no. I had no desire for any monetary gain or any elevation in stature relating to political activities.

Oh, yes, in the past I'd thought, wouldn't it be wonderful someday to go to Washington and have Quentin see to my appointment as a special counsel for some committee? My mind wandered a bit, thinking about the hearings on Senator Joe McCarthy and the tremendous job that had been done by counsel for the investigating Senate subcommittee. But that was only a thought and a wild dream, and I had mentioned that possibility to absolutely no one.

My friend Eugene Sweeney of Sweeney Tractor Company in Fargo, an older man, a good supporter of the Democratic Party, a person I could count on whenever I needed a contribution for a special cause in politics, did say to me once, "Myron, you ought to be thinking about a judgeship."

"No way, Gene," I said. "I'm not interested." Truly I was not, at that time. But that's another story.

Let's go back to the change in perspective.

Sometime in July, the week after the special election, I was working in my office and my telephone rang. The voice on the phone said, "Myron, this is Mort Wilk. I want to talk to you about something. Can you come over to my office?"

"Absolutely, Mort," I said. "I'll be over in a half an hour."

Mortimer "Mort" Wilk was a prominent citizen of Fargo, a grain merchant, a philanthropist, a member of Temple Beth El as I was, and a big supporter of the Temple. Mortimer and his wife, a very nice Norwegian lady of whom I was very fond, had two daughters. He also was a very good friend of my law partner Philip Vogel. Philip's oldest daughter, Patricia, and Mort's daughter, Karen, were best friends.

Mortimer had served in the North Dakota House of Representatives. He was a Republican but nevertheless served as an unofficial political adviser to me in some ways.

I walked over to Mort's office, sat down and we exchanged a few pleasantries. Then, out came the bomb. It hit me with a wham, like a right cross to my forehead. Mortimer said, "Myron, your partners Mart and Phil Vogel are wondering whether you are going to be a full-time politician or if you are going to be a full-time lawyer?"

A moment of silence, maybe thirty seconds. It didn't take long for me to express my decision.

"Mort," I said, "I'm going to be a full-time lawyer. I'm resigning as county chairman of the Democratic Party board immediately and I'm going to devote most of my time to my law practice."

I remembered too well what had happened during the past ten months. My production in the sense of generating work had declined about fifty percent. In the past, I had generated fees at least thirty or forty percent more than I drew. However, I knew that my production had slipped greatly. As a matter of fact, as of November of 1960, I think my total production and fees was around thirty-five thousand dollars. No wonder my partners were concerned.

I quickly put my decision into action.

I went back to the office and dictated a letter to my friends and compatriots in the Democratic Party. I said, in essence, "I'm sorry, but I no longer can continue as chairman of the Democratic Party for Cass County.

I must devote my full attention to my law practice and I'm unable to give to party matters the attention which is needed."

I also called members of the executive committee and it wasn't very long afterward that the committee held a meeting of all the precinct committeemen to accept my resignation and name Curtis Olson to succeed me.

I told my friends in the party that I would continue working in the party, and that Fritzie would continue working in the party, but to a lesser degree than in the past.

I believe I made the proper decision to step down as county chairman. Politics makes a great sideline effort, but it cannot be a main goal if a person wants to be a lawyer. I wanted to be a lawyer and I wanted to be a good one.

I've never regretted my political activity. One of the things I've always said is that before 1958, I probably knew about a thousand people in North Dakota, mostly in Fargo and Cass County, but as a result of my political activity, I probably knew something like ten or fifteen thousand people all over this state.

I want to give credit where credit is due. I pay special tribute to those persons who stuffed the envelopes for mailings, to those who walked the streets, knocked on doors, took surveys of the residents to determine who were the Democrats and who were the independents, and who needed to be brought to the polls to vote for our candidates in the elections. Party workers distributed literature. They came to the organization rallies and spread the news about the Democratic candidates and urged the citizens and their friends to vote for them.

Those people were my friends and whatever success I achieved as a political leader I owe to them.

Although I no longer carried the title of chairman of the Cass County Democratic Party, I still worked in the party in the ensuing years. Fritzie and I helped with fundraising. She ran Democratic headquarters in subsequent campaigns — that is, the fall of 1960, fall of 1962, the fall of 1964 and the fall of 1966.

Fritzie and I and others in the Democratic Party decided to have a banquet honoring Burdick in an off-election period. In 1964, somewhere in January or February. as I recall, we had gathered at the Civic Auditorium and we sold tickets at twenty-five dollars each. This was a fundraising affair and also an opportunity to pay tribute to Burdick for his good work in the Senate. Luther Hodges, U.S. Secretary of Commerce, was the main speaker. It was a very successful event. John Riley, a local Republican official, had written a letter in *The Forum* daily newspaper that said, "Don't be fooled by these banquets. You're contributing to the Democratic Party and Republicans should not attend." We called the event non-partisan, but many Republicans did come.

One incident that comes to mind is my visit with the publisher of *The Forum,* Norman Black Jr., a strong Republican who was a friend and a client of my firm. I said I'd like to have *The Forum* buy some tickets for the banquet. Black looked at me and said, "Well, Quentin is a good man. I'll take five tickets." He wrote me a check for $125, I gave him the five tickets to the banquet, and I danced on air, or it seemed like that, in walking from *The Forum* building back to my office on Broadway.

Quentin Burdick planned to run for re-election in November of 1964. Prior to that election year, Fritzie and I ruminated about an affair to raise money, honor Burdick, and attract Republican and independent voters to support Quentin. A good time would be a time before he acquired an opponent. Thus, we hatched the idea for a "nonpartisan" Burdick dinner and program. With the cooperation of the Burdick staff, we got a committee together to plan the event.

The key to success focused on *nonpartisan*. The Salute to Burdick committee was organized to *front* the affair although Fritzie and I, and the Democratic-NPL Party members did the real work.

Frank Woell of Casselton served as chairman. As I recall it, he was a relative of Bill Langer, the late Republican senator from North Dakota. Frank was the entrée to the old Bill Langer supporters.

Next came Herschel Lashkowitz, Fargo's mayor since 1954. He had rejoined the folds of the Democratic-NPL Party in North Dakota after his aborted attempt to run for governor against Guy in 1960.

Others on the committee were community leaders, professionals, farmers and businessmen, none of whom necessarily had strong ties to the Democratic-NPL party.

The big event on January 19, 1964, served as a grand kickoff for Burdick's reelection campaign that fall. The biggest problem we faced was predicting the attendance. Almost two thousand people filled the city auditorium. The guest speaker, Commerce Secretary Hodges, served as a strong attraction to the business community.

Later in the fall of 1964, I participated in that campaign. In particular, I wrote one of Burdick's effective TV campaign speeches, which was five minutes in length and was simultaneously telecast in prime time on all three Fargo TV stations.

Although I did not participate in any of Burdick's political activities after I became a federal judge in the summer of 1968, Quentin and his wife, Jocie, remained the closest of friends with Fritzie and me. Did we discuss politics? Of course.

After Quentin's death on September 8, 1992, following thirty-two years of service in the Congress, Fritzie and I played just one more role in the life of the Burdicks, getting Jocie appointed to the very short term as Quentin's successor until a special election in which Kent Conrad was elected.

That's still another story. This is about Governor George Sinner's appointment of Quentin's widow, Jocie Burdick, to a short term in the United States Senate to replace her husband until the electorate could vote on a permanent replacement for the balance of the Senate term. Only part of the story can be told now because some of the participants are still alive and their privacy needs some protection.

Of course, at this time, I was a sitting judge and could not really participate in political affairs. However, I had my opinions and I could be consulted. Employees of Quentin Burdick in his Fargo office, which was located almost adjacent to mine in the Federal Building, came to me and mentioned that Jocelyn Burdick would be a good replacement and would be a person who would keep them on the payroll for at least a short time. I made no commitment.

Some time, a day or two, after the funeral, Governor Sinner called me and said, "Myron, what do you think about my appointing Jocelyn Burdick to the U.S. Senate?" I said, "George, let me think it over and I will call you in the morning." That evening, I talked with Fritzie about the possible selection of Jocie to fill the vacancy. Fritzie was enthusiastic and said, "Absolutely. This would be a great appointment. It would help Jocie get over the grief of the death of Quentin and would be good for the whole party."

I thought about it for a while. The next morning, I called Governor Sinner and said, "I think Jocie would make an excellent person to be appointed to the vacancy." Of course, this was only a few days after Quentin's funeral and the grief was heavy in the Burdick family.

In my conversation with the governor, he mentioned that someone very close to him had wanted the appointment and he would be in big trouble with that close person if he selected someone else. However, George said, and this was an act of real political courage, "I think I can handle it and I am going to appoint Jocie, but I want to make sure she will accept that appointment before I release it to the press and public." I then talked to one of Quentin Burdick's staff and learned that, yes, Jocie would accept. I called Governor Sinner, gave him the message and reaffirmed my statement that this would be a wonderful appointment. He agreed. A short time later that day, Governor Sinner announced the appointment, Jocie said she would accept and the deed was done.

It was a good appointment. Everyone was happy about it, except, perhaps, those others who wanted the position. It saved the vacancy for a proper person to run at an appropriate time and it was a courageous move. I give great credit to Governor Sinner for his judgment and his courage to overcome personal matters in making this significant appointment. Jocie left soon thereafter to serve in the U.S. Senate for several weeks until the special election was held in January.

One other vignette goes along with the replacement of Quentin Burdick. Kent Conrad had served one term in the Senate and then declined to run for a second term because he had not succeeded in balancing the federal budget. He had promised the electorate if he did not succeed, he would not run for re-election.

Byron Dorgan had been elected in North Dakota to follow Conrad as a U.S. senator. At the funeral for Quentin, Fritzie and I met Kent Conrad and his wife, Lucy. Kent was in his last days as an elected United States senator. The situation had changed from his original view that he would not run for re-election. Fritzie and I said to Kent, "You are a logical candidate and you should run for the vacancy created by Quentin's death." For a moment, Kent seemed to answer in the negative when Fritzie said to him, "How do you like the term Senator Earl Strinden (referring to the candidate who had been defeated by Quentin in 1988 election for the U.S. Senate)?" Quentin's term ran to 1994, so whoever was elected to the vacancy would serve for approximately two more years.

Whether our words had an effect or not, I am not sure, but we do know that Kent Conrad ran and was elected. He served, not only through the Burdick period, but, in the end, for the next nineteen years until he decided not to run again when his term ended in 2012.

— CHAPTER 18 —

My Time is Your Time
Your Time is My Time (Rudy Valley, 1929)

William "Bill" Guy, starting in 1960, demonstrated what an intelligent, young, moderately liberal person could accomplish as governor of North Dakota.

Governor Guy headed an effective, efficient and fair administration. It was time to celebrate his good works. That event came about during a very auspicious period for our state and our country. The date was May 13, 1967, in Guy's seventh year as governor. The theme, "My time, your time," came from Bill's conduct bringing the state of North Dakota in sync with most of the country that followed daylight-saving time. Bill's action to preserve daylight-saving time was a courageous move. Most farmers cried foul: "Our cows don't give milk on daylight-saving time; neither do our chickens lay eggs on daylight time." Bill stood fast! Thus the theme for the party.

I sold a lot of tickets. Again, the event was advertised as a "nonpartisan" tribute to Governor Guy. Fritzie played a prominent role in arranging a present for the Guys, a grandfather clock to be given, as I recall it, to Bill's wife, Jean.

Fritzie and I needed to estimate the crowd. We calculated that the event drew more than two thousand attendees to the Fargo Civic Auditorium.

Guy had recently served or was then serving as chairman of the national conference of state governors. He was held in high regard across the country by the press and others.

The nonpartisan (sort of) organizing committee included Floyd Poyzer, the owner or manager of a grain elevator in Amenia, and a good friend of the Guys. At the affair, on behalf of Bill's friends and neighbors, Floyd presented Bill with an enlarged picture of a farming scene that had been on a now-rare two-cent postage stamp issued in 1898. The rural people of Cass County turned out in mass to honor him.

Vice President Hubert Humphrey arrived in Fargo in the early afternoon. Almost immediately, he made an appearance before North Dakota State University students. He wasn't greeted warmly. The campus displayed sign after sign opposing the Vietnam War. Many were carried by students. In his remarks on campus, Humphrey defended President Johnson's handling of Vietnam.

Humphrey's reception at the Guy appreciation dinner was entirely different. No signs. The crowd was friendly and appreciative. One could sense and feel the warmth and respect and high regard of the audience for the vice president of the United States.

Humphrey responded with a wonderful speech praising Guy as a great governor. He spoke of the promise of freedom in America and its message to the world.

Humphrey a day earlier had visited the Minnesota Iron Range country in northeastern Minnesota, an area that has always been a hotbed of Democratic Party support in Minnesota. However, the vice president faced some hostile people because of the Vietnam War and had even been spat upon there.

But the overflow crowd in the Fargo city auditorium was different. Hubert spoke for over an hour. The audience paid close attention to every word and the evening proved to be a huge success. Humphrey freely mixed with the crowd and shook a lot of hands. I spoke to the vice president and received a nice gift, a pair of gold cufflinks adorned with the vice presidential seal.

The gathering gave Bill Guy a big boost as governor. He continued to serve in that high office through 1972.

Young Myron

Myron playing high school football

Photos 1

Morris, Myron and Lena Bright, 1943.

Graduation from Eveleth Junior College, 1939.

Myron Bright in Army Air Corps uniform, World War II.

Myron H. Bright

Judge Bright at the World War II Memorial, 2007

Myron and Fritzie married in 1946.

University of Minnesota Law Review staff, 1946-47.

Myron's sister, Mabel, and Lena Bright, 1956.

Myron Bright, John F. Kennedy and Joe Poer at the Burdick Birthday Party.

Myron Bright, Quentin Burdick, Joe Poer, John F. Kennedy, John Murphy.

Lt. Gov. Charles Tighe, unknown woman, Fritzie Bright, Scott Anderson (behind her), P.W. Lanier, and Governor William Guy.

Fritzie and Myron Bright with Senator Quentin Burdick and President Lyndon Johnson in the White House.

Judge Bright sworn into the court, August 16, 1968. Left to right, Myron Bright, Judge Charles Vogel, Judge George Register, and Judge Harry Blackmun (who later became Supreme Court Justice).

Brothers Leo, Joe, Myron, and Roy Bright, 1972.

Son Josh,
Myron Bright,
daughter Dinah.

Chris Golding (Judge Bright's son-in-law), Justice Ruth Bader Ginsburg, Myron Bright in 2013.

James Dean Walker and Judge Bright in 2013.

United States Court of Appeals for the Eighth Circuit, 2013.
(Photo by Trotter Photo)

SECTION THREE

— CHAPTER 19 —

The Judgeship

How did I become a federal judge? Strange circumstances indeed. I once stated that, at least for me, becoming a U.S. Circuit Court judge could be compared with throwing a jigsaw puzzle of one thousand pieces out an airplane window and having the pieces come together as a completed puzzle upon hitting the ground. An exaggeration, of course, but that's an idea of a lawyer's odds.

I had never thought about my legal career extending anywhere except serving as a lawyer, particularly a trial and appellate lawyer. I considered myself to be very good at what I did and I loved my work and my association with two able, friendly partners, Philip and Mart Vogel.

The scene shifts to June of 1965. After a dragged-out argument with Fritzie about a summer vacation, we finally agreed to take the children to Washington, D.C., to see the sites in the capital of our country.

I recall the event clearly. I'm driving our white 1965 Chrysler four-door sedan on the Pennsylvania Turnpike when Fritzie speaks these eventful words:

Fritzie: Myron, when we get to D.C., why don't you ask Quentin about a judgeship?

Myron: What the hell do I want a judgeship for? I'm having too much fun as a trial lawyer.

Fritzie: Listen, Myron, I want a live husband, not a dead trial lawyer. End of conversation.

Fritzie, in her dead trial lawyer comment, referred to the mental strain upon a trial lawyer in actually trying lawsuits.

Yes, I experienced that. I could easily lose ten pounds during the week of a trial. Often during a lawsuit, I'd work a sixteen-hour day, but it was challenging and fun.

Fritzie and I visited Burdick at his office in the Senate Office building. "Quentin," I said. "If a judgeship comes up, I might be interested."

Quentin gave me a sort of half-smile, quizzical look and said, "That's interesting. You are the only one who has asked me except my brother Gene" (Eugene Burdick, Quentin's younger brother, was serving as a North Dakota state district judge). Quentin added, "It would be political suicide for me to have a part in appointing my brother."

Nothing more was said about a federal judgeship, although the gem of an idea had been planted in my mind. However, I didn't think much about it for a few years.

In late November or early December 1967, Charles Vogel, the chief judge of the Eighth Circuit U.S. Court of Appeals, and the older brother of my law partners, Philip and Mart Vogel, announced that he would take senior status in early 1968. Thus an opening would exist.

As I look back over the years, these are the puzzle pieces, by year, that fitted together to make me a federal judge.

First: About 1955, Quentin Burdick and I became best friends when I came to his medical rescue on his collapsing in state court in Minot.

Second: 1954, getting elected precinct committeeman for the Democratic Party on the flip of a coin.

Third: March or April 1958, nominating Quentin for Congress at the Democratic-NPL Party convention.

Fourth: 1958, becoming Cass County Democratic chairman and spearheading Quentin's successful campaign for Congress.

Fifth: 1960, getting Bill Guy the nomination for governor of North Dakota on the Democratic-NPL Party ticket. He served twelve years in that office.

Sixth: 1960, providing my and Fritzie's brains and efforts to Quentin's campaign to become a U.S. senator, and along with the John Murphy family, the Burdick children, and many, many others putting together the Burdick Birthday Party on June 19, 1960; and helping to arrange John F. Kennedy's appearance at that event.

Seventh: 1960-68, continuing as a best friend to Burdick, now a U.S.

senator, and participating in Democratic-NPL Party activities of various kinds until the spring of 1968.

Eighth: Late 1967 and 1968. Additionally, I thought it would look sort of strange if Quentin Burdick nominated someone other than Myron Bright for the judicial vacancies, because Myron Bright was considered his close friend and ally.

I contacted Quentin. He said, "OK, I'll recommend you to President Johnson for that vacancy."

Now, my ambition started building. As I think back on my thoughts, I recall saying to myself, "I'm really not that interested, but because I'm Quentin's best friend, it would surely look strange and a put-down if Quentin recommended someone else."

The die became cast. Now, I wanted the judgeship. I called my two partners, Philip and Mart, to meet with me so I could tell them of my situation. Neither was happy about my leaving the firm.

Mart said, "Myron, why would you want to become a federal judge? It will be like withdrawing from the human race and living in an ivory tower."

In that remark, Mart referred to Charles Vogel's service as both a federal district judge from 1941-1955, and as a circuit judge from 1955-1968. Charles lived a sort of sheltered life, doing only judging and not much of anything else.

However Mart and Phil assured me of their support to obtain the position of federal circuit judge.

Burdick announced his support for me. Then Milton Young, the senior senator from North Dakota and a Republican, declared that he was sending Eugene Burdick's name to the president. I think Young submitted Eugene's name to embarrass Quentin and to ingratiate himself with Eugene's friends in western North Dakota. Young asserted that many lawyers in western North Dakota supported Judge Burdick's nomination. He added, though, that if the president nominated me, he would support my nomination.

During the interval before President Johnson made a choice, I said to Quentin, "I don't want to come between you and your brother in this judgeship appointment."

The response by Quentin, "Forget it." Quentin also told me later that to maintain peace in the family, he gave Eugene an oil well Quentin had inherited from their father, Usher Burdick.

Some of the amusing and not amusing incidents in my campaign for the nomination included comments by my friend Senator Burdick. Fritzie and I had literally worked our minds and hearts out in Quentin's various election campaigns. Many of the Democratic-NPL Party people believed that the contribution we made to Quentin's winning of the Senate seat had been important, crucial. So in the process, it almost knocked me for a loop when Quentin said to me, "Get the party support for the judgeship." I thought: *and after all this!*

Well, I did get the support of almost every major person in the Democratic-NPL Party, including state chairman, national committee persons and others. Then, almost each week during January, February, March and April 1968, I would ask Quentin to see the president about my appointment. Quentin's stock answer generally went like this, "The president knows where to find me. I don't need to seek him out." I got the idea that maybe Quentin was not too keen about seeing me get out of politics, which would be my situation when serving as a federal judge.

In the campaign to become a federal circuit judge, letters of support became important. Some of those were truly heartwarming. One amusing letter came from Bismarck lawyer Bill Murray, who had served as Lyndon Johnson's North Dakota chairman in 1960 when LBJ sought the Democratic Party's presidential nomination.

Murray had previously run for a vacancy on the North Dakota Supreme Court. I helped his campaign by raising money and support from Fargo lawyers. So I expected a return favor. Instead, Bill wrote that he was backing Robert Vogel (no relative of my partners) for the position even though Vogel, a superb person, had not been mentioned for the judgeship by Senator Burdick or Senator Young, and therefore could not then be considered. An appropriate comment might be: With friends like that, who needs enemies.

Commencing from this period of time, the campaign was on to obtain the nomination. My law partners, Mart Vogel, Philip Vogel and Charles Wattam, contacted their Democratic and Republican friends in the legal profession asking them to write the president in support of Myron Bright to be the next federal circuit judge. Some friends, including Jay Phillips, a wealthy industrialist from Minneapolis, wrote to Hubert Humphrey in my support. I personally saw my old law school classmate, Orville

Freeman, then secretary of agriculture. He assured me that he would talk to LBJ on my behalf.

Believe it or not, Judge Burdick thought he would receive the appointment right up to the end. I say this is because Eugene Burdick and George Sinner, later governor of North Dakota, visited during a meeting of the State Board of Higher Education. Eugene told George that the federal judgeship would go to himself. Dreaming!

During this interim period until the nomination was actually made, I talked to Quentin about another possible scenario. I really wanted to be a federal trial judge as a first choice, rather than on the circuit appeals court. So after talking to federal Judge Ronald N. Davies, who was due to take senior status in a few years, I suggested a two-way appointment — name Davies to the circuit bench and appoint me to his vacancy for the time being. Then when Davies became a senior circuit judge, I could be appointed to the circuit court.

Quentin said, "Forget it, it's too complicated."

But unknown to me, there were other matters at work affecting the nomination and those matters relate to Robert F. Kennedy. I turn to RFK's relationship with the Brights and, in part, interrupt discussing the quest for the judgeship, except as RFK played a role in my appointment.

— CHAPTER 20 —

RFK and the Bright Family

The relationship between the Bright family and Robert Kennedy played an important role in my becoming a federal judge. In 1968, I first learned about the RFK role after my visit to Washington, D.C., on or about May 8, 1968, for my confirmation hearing before the U.S. Senate.

I met Robert (Bobby) sometime during his role as attorney general in the John Kennedy administration. Bobby visited Governor Guy at the state Capitol in Bismarck. I made a special trip to meet him at the Governor's Residence. I don't remember much about the visit except that I enjoyed meeting Bobby, found him very pleasant and down to earth.

The scene shifted to that visit my family and I made to D.C. in June of 1965 when the judgeship subject came up with Quentin. At that time, Bobby served as a senator from New York. Upon our arrival in Washington, our first stop was Senator Burdick's office. The time was probably near 5:00 p.m. Both my children, Dinah and Josh, pulled on Quentin's jacket saying, "We want to meet Bobby. We want to meet Bobby."

Here's the response to us by Quentin: "We have a vote coming in a few minutes. Bobby and I sit next to each other. I will ask him if he can meet your family. If the answer is yes, I'll give you a wave with my hand. I'll put you in the balcony of the Senate Chambers. If we meet, it will be on the second floor in the Senate visitors room."

Quentin took us to the Senate Gallery. What a thrill and spectacle. We watched the senators take their seats and cast their roll-call vote. We particularly had our eyes on Quentin and Bobby. Burdick gave the high sign.

After the vote, we walked one flight of stairs to the visitors room and Bobby, one of his aides, Quentin, my wife, my children and I met Bobby. What a pleasure.

During our conversation, daughter Dinah said to Bobby, "You know we sang for your brother." She referred to the 1960 campaign appearance in Fargo by John F. Kennedy in September of that year.

Bobby got a far-away look in his eye, then took out a blue Senate pad about four inches square and wrote, "Dinah I hope you will sing for me too, soon."

So, in June of 1965, that was his unofficial announcement that he would run for president.

His aide took a picture of Bobby and my family; a print and the original of the above message is kept in the Kennedy Museum in the Boston area.

Let the scene change. It is now a day in 1968, April 15. Kennedy is campaigning in the Midwest seeking the nomination to run for president as the candidate of the Democratic Party.

Earlier that day, RFK had been in Sioux Falls, where Senator George McGovern introduced him to the audience as a man who would make a great president.

Bobby flew into Fargo that evening for an appearance at the Civic Auditorium, capacity about thirty-five hundred people.

My name previously had been sent to the White House by Burdick as a possible appointee to the U.S. Court of Appeals for the Eighth Circuit, so I was abstaining from any partisan political activity. But Fritzie had played a role in making arrangements for the RFK appearance.

My two children, Dinah, then age fifteen, and Josh, age twelve, were great fans of Bobby. So the whole family, all four of us, came to the auditorium about an hour early. Bobby was scheduled to appear at about 8:00 p.m., but he arrived late, around 9:30 p.m. The auditorium at 8:00 p.m. was jam-packed and almost full. It reached capacity shortly thereafter. The fire chief would not allow standing-room persons. I looked outside. The doors became closed. I made an estimate — thirty-five hundred people inside, ten thousand people outside screaming: "We want to see Bobby."

Fritzie and I occupied a seat near the control room, at the opposite end from the stage. Fritzie had found seats for Josh and Dinah at the front. But that changed. We moved them to the rear of the auditorium because of the bomb threat described below.

The Fargo police in numbers came to the auditorium because a bomb threat had been phoned to the Police Department. No announcement of this danger was communicated to the audience. Good thing, because there could have been a panic.

The police made a thorough search, especially at the front of the auditorium and around the stage, and they found nothing.

A few minutes before 9:30 p.m. Bobby arrived accompanied by his aide — Frank Mankiewicz — who also served as his press secretary. Several policeman surrounded Bobby and Mankiewicz and literally battered their way through the crowd into the auditorium.

I was at the front doors to greet my longtime friend. I overheard the following:

Policeman to Bobby and aide: "We've had a bomb threat, but can't find anything."

Bobby: "We're going in." And they did, to absolute bedlam, wild cheering.

After an introduction, by whom I can't recall, Bobby took the microphone. After making one statement he was greeted with loud cheers from a standing crowd. The audience loved it. They cheered after almost every spoken sentence.

Bobby looked tired. He had engaged in a full day of activity with various airplane stops, including the one in Sioux Falls.

After the speech, Bobby left the auditorium standing on a flatbed trailer pulled by a truck with a police escort. Thousands of people lined the streets on the route cheering him.

What a smashing appearance. I harbored no doubt in my mind that Bobby would be the next president. But a few weeks later, it was over when he was gunned down by that terrible, misguided Sirhan Sirhan. I believe the history of our country would have been radically different and for the better had RFK lived.

This concludes my political history because only a few weeks later, on June 7, 1968, I received my appointment as a federal circuit judge. It was a time of mixed gladness and sadness as, coincidentally with my appointment, the country mourned the death of Robert F. Kennedy.

I did not know it at the time, but I found out later when I was in D.C. for my hearings that the Bobby Kennedy campaign in the Midwest resulted in my becoming the federal circuit judge rather than Senator McGovern's choice, Francis Dunn, from South Dakota.

Here's the gist of the story from the syndicated newspaper column of Rowland Evans and Robert Novak:

> President Johnson's appointment of Myron H. Bright as U.S. Court of Appeals judge for the Eighth Circuit concealed a tangled web of presidential politics, patronage and revenge.
>
> When Chief Judge Charles J. Vogel, a native of North Dakota, announced his intention to retire early this year, Sen. George McGovern of South Dakota, one of Robert F. Kennedy's closest political friends, strongly recommended a South Dakota judge [Francis Dunn] as Vogel's replacement. U.S. Attorney General Ramsey Clark promised McGovern the appointment to Judge Dunn.
>
> But on April 25, nine days after McGovern effusively introduced Kennedy to a political rally in South Dakota, the senator's office received a telephone call from the Justice Department that the matter of the appointment had been taken out of Justice by the White House and that Dunn was no longer under consideration. Later that same day, the President formally nominated Bright, a North Dakota lawyer without any judicial experience to the Vogel vacancy.
>
> Top Democrats in South Dakota ... concluded that McGovern was being punished for giving Kennedy such obvious help in the South Dakota primary.

The truth of that story had evidenced itself to me while I was in Washington for my Senate committee hearing. The White House counsel told Fritzie and me that my appointment had been made in the White House.

— CHAPTER 21 —

Appointment and Confirmation Meeting With President Lyndon Baines Johnson

Now to a very important date: April 25, 1968. I am defending a lawsuit in district court in Wahpeton, North Dakota. I had completed the trial before noon and my client's daughter and I got together for lunch at the Wahpeton Elks Club. I heard my name being called to answer the telephone. Here's my recollection of the phone conversation:

"Hello, this is Myron Bright."

The response came in a gravelly, somewhat hesitant voice: "This is Gif (Gifford) Herron of *The Fargo Forum*. I just received an AP [Associated Press] dispatch as follows: President Lyndon B. Johnson today nominated Myron Bright of Fargo to be a judge of the United States Court of Appeals for the Eighth Circuit."

I answered in one word, "Wow."

I remember the call well. What a thrill. In fact, a real bang when my tire blew on my way back to Fargo. I found Fritzie playing bridge at the Jerome Siegel residence. After a joyous time of celebrating there, we headed for home.

This was hot news. The telephone kept ringing with people offering congratulations.

I remember one call well. Albert Teigen, a real character in Fargo, called and wanted to paint my house. I said no. He asked me what the judge's job paid. I said seventeen thousand dollars, although the compensation then was thirty-three thousand per year. He responded with a whistle.

The Forum gave the announcement front-page coverage.

Quentin didn't let any grass grow underfoot. On May 1, he arranged for my nomination to be heard by a Senate Judiciary subcommittee on May 8.

Time was flying, but I had an unfortunate interruption. While playing pingpong about a week before the hearing, I sprained an ankle. I didn't want to travel to D.C. on crutches. A member of the athletic department at North Dakota State University who did the taping for football players taped up my ankle. I then was able to walk without crutches.

So off to Washington went Fritzie and me. The first order of the day was to attend a hearing before the subcommittee, chaired by Senator James Eastland, who also chaired the Judiciary Committee. Quentin spoke on my behalf.

Eastland asked no questions, but I thought he might bite his cigar in two when Quentin mentioned my being president of Temple Beth El, the Jewish synagogue in Fargo.

Of course, I was confirmed.

Three other incidents stand out. The first: deputy attorney general Warren Christopher (later secretary of state in the Clinton presidency) treated me very warmly. Warren was born in North Dakota, but left the state at age seven. But Ramsey Clark, the attorney general, gave me what may be called a cold shoulder.

The second was a visit to the Supreme Court. I felt that I should meet Justice Byron White. So I arranged that for the morning of May 9th. I recall sitting outside his office awaiting his call.

The secretary took me into the office of the justice. At first I saw no one, just a desk piled high with books. Then this tall man arose, put out his hand for a handshake, and announced, "I'm Byron White."

I replied, "That's funny, I'm Myron Bright." We shook hands and became friends from then on.

The big event of that process in Washington, D.C., was the visit with President Johnson. I dictated the following report of that visit shortly after the event:

A VISIT WITH THE PRESIDENT
May 8, 1968

12:20 p.m.

Fritzie and I are at Senator Burdick's Office getting a last gulp of coffee. We look at the clock. It is 12:20. Maybe the traffic is heavy. We better get going. We have a meeting with the president of the United States at 12:45 p.m. this date.

12:25 p.m.

We're a little early. We arrive at the southwest gate. A tough-looking officer pokes his head in the car. "What do you want?" We explain we're Mr. and Mrs. Myron Bright and we have an appointment with the president of the United States at 12:45. His face changes. There is a look of courtesy.

He asks for identification. I take out my wallet and pull out my Elks card. The seal seems to be official enough and we are passed into the gates at the southwest gate into a small hallway where another officer stops us, asks for our identification and checks are names against the register. This time I pull out my membership card in the Democratic-NPL Party of North Dakota signed by Larry Erickson. This seems to do the trick and we are ushered into the basement of the White House and asked to take a seat on a beautiful, black leather couch. Fritzie and I look at each other with a slight smile. I move over to the corner, and we both light a cigarette. A few minutes later, a young colored elevator operator greets us and asks us to accompany him into the elevator where we are escorted up to the first floor on the west wing of the White House and brought into the room known as the Fish Room.

Fritzie, please describe the Fish Room.

Fritzie: The Fish Room is a rectangular room with an oval shape at one end, no windows, but four doors leading into this room. It is furnished in a red and white motif in period furniture, very tastefully done. There is a bouquet of fresh garden flowers in the center of a table which seats ten people, with chairs drawn around it. It had a speaker's dais at one end, with microphones attached, right in front of the fireplace. The pictures hanging on the wall were beautiful oils done all by American artists, as far as we could discern. There was a framed document of Thomas Jefferson's on one of the desks in which he described the Fahrenheit thermometer and the botanical sciences to the then president of the United States. They had a carved whaler done in whale bone under a glass case on the other desk at the other side of the room.

The furniture was not formal. There was a bright red carpet, oval carpet, on the cork floor. The gold key cornice around the entire room, which was, by the way, painted a beautiful shade of beige — kind of rosy-beige. The furniture was done in red, with white relief. There were chairs drawn up around a coffee table, which Mike and I, after looking at all of the objects in the room, sat ourselves down. There were, by the way, on either side of the mantle two gold urns, which looked as though they might be part of the Monroe collection, though we didn't inquire, but it looked like the type of thing we had seen in the formal dining room in the downstairs when we toured the White House some years before.

Myron: Well, I'll slip in here and I mention over the fireplace was an original Remington painting of a cowboy and on one of the walls there was a mountain scene with blue corn flowers. I was very much impressed by these three paintings as well as the other paintings, and I thought it was somewhat appropriate, since one of them was a painting with Indians on it. I thought, what a most appropriate room for someone from North Dakota to await an interview with the president.

In the meantime, we're anxiously awaiting the arrival of Senator Burdick, who had arranged the interview, and we're worried because it is now 12:45 and we are due to meet the president. The door opens. A young man in his late twenties comes in and greets us. His name is Larry Temple, and he is a handsome, young man of about six feet tall, a graduate of the University of Texas Law School, and he explains that he is the liaison representative with the Justice Department.

Mr. Temple congratulates Fritzie and me and explains that he has seen the FBI report and the other pertinent data in my file. We make small talk for a few minutes, and finally our friend, Quentin Burdick, the junior senator of North Dakota, arrives. He has just been entertaining some Farmers Union members and he had rushed away from lunch to join us at the White House.

Temple leaves after a few moments and Quentin and Fritzie and I talk about the room and smile at each other, and a few moments later, a young man with horn-rimmed glasses, about five feet seven inches tall, comes in and I guess that this is probably Mr. James Jones, who is the appointments secretary to the president. Jones introduces himself to Fritzie and me and Senator Burdick. I have heard about this young man, and read about him, since he is at the right hand of the seat of power. He is a friend of Scott Anderson of Fargo and Larry Erickson of Minot.

We talked for a few moments. Jones asks us to come into the president's anteroom in the White House, and we enter that room. Jones pulls off his mantle over his bookcase an object that he looks at with pride and says, "This is a present from my friend Larry Erickson from Minot." Fritzie, take over the description of the Erickson present.

Fritzie: The Erickson present was a ceramic donkey about eight inches tall with an inscription on the donkey.

The anteroom had one secretary; I take it Mr. Jones' secretary, seated at a desk, a large telephone complex. It was done in blue and white. Very modern office furniture, but it did have two provincial chairs, also done in blue with a walnut finish, drawn up to a very small fireplace. We waited for a little while taking with Mr. Jones, and then we were told that the president would see us as soon as he finished his phone call. The White House photographer was with us, had three cameras strapped around his neck, and it looked very official and efficient.

We were then ushered into a small hall, and while we were waiting for the president to finish, Senator Burdick showed us a side office; I believe the room was once a cloakroom, but the president had fixed it up as a little side office. He has his telephone console in there, three portable TV sets, all turned on, tuned into different channels, it was explained to us, and two chairs drawn up. The room was done with velvet portiere drapes in green with an off-white wall. It was very attractive. A very cozy room. Many personal pictures and mementoes hanging on the wall. We couldn't see all of them because we just glanced into this small room.

Myron: Tension and excitement mounted. We waited with bated breath. We could hear the president dictating to his secretary and Mr. Jones said, "Well, we'd better step out again," and so back into the waiting room we went. We sat for just a few moments, and then the telephone rang and Mr. Jones' secretary advised that we should go in. Fritzie went first, I followed, and Senator Burdick was behind me.

The president greeted us just as we entered his office, which I believe was the Oval Room. The president was dressed in a blue-gray suit. He is a handsome and imposing person, much warmer in person than he appears on television. He greeted Fritzie, he congratulated me, and he shook hands with Senator Burdick. In the meantime, the photographer is busy taking pictures from all angles. The president was very warm in his congratulations, and it was obvious that he knew the entire background on the appointment. Fritzie, maybe you would like to describe the room. I did notice one thing, and that was the Kennedy rocker in the room, but, perhaps you will do a better job of describing the furnishings than I can. Frankly, my eyes were on the president at all times.

Fritzie: The room is a large oval-shaped room. It was done in off-white. There was a very massive desk at the right as you enter, which is the president's desk. On the floor was a large oval green rug, with the Presidential Seal in the center of the rug. The sitting room furniture, on the left-hand side as you enter, was done in off-white to match the walls. I did not notice the wall hangings or anything, except the Presidential Seal, and the flags behind the desk. I must say that I, too, was entranced with this man, who is our president.

Myron: The president then gave us the rose garden tour. He said North Dakota has good-looking women and grabbed Fritzie by her arm. The two of them walked out of the French doors to the White House porch overlooking the rose garden, and the senator and I followed.

In the meantime, the photographer was busily shooting pictures. I wish I could remember everything that was said. The president remarked on the flowers, which were very beautiful. It was a lovely sunshiny day. Fritzie, maybe you would like to describe a little bit more of our rose garden tour. Take over.

Fritzie: The rose garden. There were not any roses in bloom, but the formal part of the garden was closely cropped, the grass was lush green and the little fruit trees were all budded out in their green leaves, though there were no blossoms apparent. It was a very quiet and very peaceful place and I remarked to the president that this must be a wonderful spot to get some peace of mind for himself and his very arduous task as our president. At that moment, he poked his head in one of the offices on the side of the porch and said to his secretary, "You know I'm not going down to that first appointment, but will you arrange to set up the next meeting in the garden?"

So I think maybe my suggestion that it was peaceful — he probably hadn't thought about this before or for a while — he decided to hold his next appointment in the garden. It was a beautiful spot and I do remember that all the time he was talking about North Dakota.

As we were walking on the porch toward the President's Office, the president expressed regret that we had missed the judicial reception at the White House the previous evening. He said, "Senator, you should have called me. You don't have to stand on ceremony with me." He then turned to us, and said, "You'll be coming back to Washington to see us." (Was this a hint of the future?)

Myron: We then walked back into the President's Office and, in the meantime, the photographer is busily taking pictures. Incidentally, the senator remarked on North Dakota cattle and spoke of beautiful cattle and, also, again of beautiful women. When we got back into his office, the president slid behind the desk and he said that he wanted to give us something to remember the visit. He said that a bronze cast had been made for a meeting in Uruguay, and he gave Fritzie a bronze cast medal for one's desk with a likeness of the president on the face of the medallion.

He also gave Fritzie two White House pencils and he handed one to Senator Burdick. He then said, "Well, judge, I can't give you this because you're going to be out of politics," but he gave Fritzie a lapel pin with LBJ on it. After again congratulating us, and after we had expressed our appreciation to the president for his action in appointing me to the Eighth Circuit Court of Appeals, the president made this statement:

"When I greet and meet the district judges, I tell them not to forget the struggles that their fathers had." Next the president said, "However, when I appoint a circuit judge, I tell the circuit judge not to forget their United States senator who put her or him there."

The president said, "You know, Mr. Bright, that the man responsible for your appointment was Senator Burdick." I told the president that I recognized that and I appreciated it very much.

It is obvious that the president is very fond of Senator Quentin Burdick.

As we were walking out of his office, toward the reception room, the president said, "You've got a good man there." He said, "Furthermore, when you're a circuit judge, while you can't be active in politics, you better get your cousins and kinsmen to remember the man who got you where you are."

The president followed us into the reception area, and he said, "Mr. Bright, you have a senator with a great deal of courage and integrity. Your senator selected you over his own brother. That is a difficult thing to do."

The president wished us luck and Fritzie and I said our goodbyes.

This day had been the thrill of a lifetime. Take over, Fritzie. I think we were both somewhat stunned and thrilled all the way back from the White House to the Senate Office Building. Do you want to make a few further comments on the visit?

Fritzie: Yes, it was a wonderful day. It gave you a feeling that this really is a great country we live in and that our government and the people who run our government are there because they are qualified to be there and that really, we are in pretty good hands. It was, also, a day that I hope, when our children play or read this record sometime in the future, that they will be able to share some of the thrills and some of the wonderful things that happened to their dad and me on May 8, 1968.

Later, Fritzie wrote two letters to President Johnson and received replies from him.

— CHAPTER 22 —

My Inauguration

I titled this chapter "Inauguration," although it is ordinarily called an induction. This is the story of my confirmation to a federal judgeship by the U.S. Senate and the period between June 6, 1968, when I received my appointment, and when I actually took the oath and was sworn in as a federal circuit judge two months later, on August 16, 1968.

Decisions had to be made, like where was I to office, when should I start my judgeship and many others. First, I determined that I would stay with the law firm and complete whatever legal work there was for me to do. Next, I decided to start my career as a renter in the Stern's Building on Broadway, adjacent to the Vogel Law Firm office. I wasn't going to move very far. I hired a great young lawyer for a law clerk, Dennis Kelly, a Notre Dame graduate.

Finally, I set August 16, 1968, as the date for my induction. The ceremony took place in the Federal Courthouse in Fargo. My immediate family plus brother Roy from Hawaii and his son John came, as well as my brother Joe and his wife, Rochelle, brother Leo and Billie Jean Bright, and brother-in-law Harry Manfield. Harry's wife, my sister, Mabel, was not in attendance.

Many judges attended. From the federal bench were Judge Charles J. Vogel, presiding; Judge Harry Blackmun and Judge Gerald Heaney, Eighth Circuit judges; and Chief Justice Obert C. Teigen of the North Dakota Supreme Court. Also the following federal district judges: Chief Judge Edward J. Devitt, St. Paul; Chief Judge George Register of Bismarck, North

Dakota; and Judge Ronald N. Davies of Fargo.

The courtroom was jammed. The hall outside the courtroom held hundreds in standing room. The attendees were friends from every part of North Dakota and many from the nearby cities in western Minnesota. I'll never forget one sentence in Senator Burdick's presentation. With a somewhat sad look in his eyes, he concluded his talk with the words, "Good-bye Mike, hello judge."

He and I knew our relationship would never be the same. Now we would be friends, not political colleagues.

We held a reception sponsored by the Cass County Bar Association at the nearby Elks Club. The report was that fifteen hundred people attended.

Wow! What an occasion.

So now Myron is a judge. Let's examine some of the decisions and perhaps explain them in terms of his background and his philosophy of life. On to the cases!

SECTION FOUR

— CHAPTER 23 —

Stand Up and Be Counted — Acceptance, Rejection, Vindication

My introduction to the Eighth Circuit occurred in September 1968. I was assigned to sit with two highly regarded and experienced judges, M. C. (for Charles) Matthes of St. Louis and Floyd R. Gibson of Kansas City, Missouri. C for Charlie, as we all affectionately called him, had been appointed by President Eisenhower in 1958. He was a kind, friendly person and a very good judge. Floyd Gibson initially had served as a federal district judge, appointed by JFK, and then, after a few years, received an appointment to the Circuit Court from LBJ in 1965.

For the first three days, we got along fine in our decision-making — no basic disagreements. Then came oral arguments and the case of *William Creighton Vaughn v. United States* (1968), a young man convicted of draft evasion who claimed he should have been classified as a conscientious objector and thus not obligated to serve in the American armed forces. Vaughn appealed that conviction.

Let me set the stage for testing Judge Bright — I must either agree with the experienced fellow judges and sustain the conviction, or disagree and show myself as a loner and probably wrong in dissent.

The incidents described occurred between 1964 and 1966, when the defendant Vaughn claimed to be a conscientious objector and he went through the proceedings of the Selective Service Act to try to prove his position, which was denied.

The question in this case was interesting.

Vaughn had initially been classified as 1-A, eligible for the draft. Later, he claimed to be a conscientious objector. He wrote a letter as follows to the Douglas County draft board in Omaha. Here are his main points:

> Dear Sirs:
>
> I request a change in classification from my present I-A to that of a conscientious objector. For me, participation in the armed services is unethical. Here are a few of my reasons.
>
> First, I believe war is outmoded. As circumstances exist today, war means complete annihilation. There is no possibility of either party gaining in an armed conflict today … The public must be educated to this fact and this is a duty far above the supposed duty to serve in the armed services.
>
> Second, killing, I believe, is immoral whenever that is our intention. Therefore to serve as part of a war effort is against any personal ethics … is capital punishment.
>
> My third reason has been alluded to in the previous sentences. That from the point of view of expediency passive resistance is much more effective.
>
> One of the freedoms I am interested in preserving is the freedom of conscience. My principles seem to be the same as Christian principles, for Christ himself said "He who takes up the sword shall perish by the sword," and "turn thou the other cheek." When will these principles become meaningful to all?
>
> Sincerely yours
> /s/ William C. Vaughn

Judge Matthes, Judge Gibson and Judge Bright engaged in a good discussion in conference after the oral argument in this case.

As a new judge, I had the temerity to suggest that maybe there was something to Vaughn's position. Maybe you didn't have to belong to a church, maybe you didn't have to have a recognized belief in an organized religion to be a conscientious objector. I felt that there might have been enough here so that the draft board should have taken another look at Vaughn's contention and his claim to be a conscientious objector.

I felt that Vaughn stated a commitment of conscience opposed to war in any form. Further, his letter evidenced at least in part a moral commitment superior to those arising from any human relationship. His belief, which he equated with Christian principles and Christ's message, paralleled the orthodox belief in God of one who could qualify for the exemption.

I was the new judge on the block, writing a dissent in an important case in which my colleagues disagreed. What should I do? I wrote a dissenting opinion. After reading my dissent, they may have thought: Is Bright a troublemaker in this court or is he really a sound judge?

Well, I was eventually vindicated.

Vaughn's counsel petitioned the Supreme Court for a writ of certiorari. The Supreme Court granted the writ and held the case for review. At the same time, the case, *Welsh v. United States,* (June 15, 1970), was presented to the Supreme Court. The Supreme Court reversed *Welsh* and then sent *Vaughn* back to the Court of Appeals for the Eighth Circuit for reconsideration in light of the *Welsh* case.

Here's a part of the August 6, 1970, letter that Judge Matthes wrote to Judge Gibson and Judge Bright:

> Dear Judges:
>
> As you know, the Supreme Court granted certiorari and summarily vacated our judgment in the above case. Mr. Tucker [clerk of court] has received a copy of the mandate remanding the case to us for further consideration in light of *Welsh v. United States,* which was decided on June 15, 1970.
>
> I have again read *Welsh* and our majority and minority opinions in *Vaughn*. I am satisfied that the beliefs of Vaughn bring him within the teachings of the Supreme Court in *Welsh*. This being the situation, I have concluded that we should vacate the judgment of conviction and remand the case to the district court with directions to dismiss the indictment.

It took a couple of years for this vindication, but after that, I think that my decisions and my views were duly respected by my colleagues. Such a vindication doesn't happen very often. I was most fortunate to have it occur on the Eighth Circuit. It made a difference in my judicial life.

My tolerance for religious views of others had been with me for many years and entered into my decision-making in *Vaughn*.[9]

— CHAPTER 24 —

Woosley:
Justice Will Be Done—I'll Find a Way

During my judging years, I made close friends with Richard Sheppard Arnold, my judicial colleague of Little Rock, Arkansas. We served together on many cases between 1980 and September of 2004, when he died.

Richard, my wife, Fritzie, and I engaged in continuing argument about the proposition of "what should a judge do?" In other words, what was a judge's job or task? This question also focused on the idea of determining "what is justice?" Fritzie would say to Richard, "You're a judge. Your job is to do justice."

Richard's stock response came out this way, "I don't do justice; I follow the law. If justice results, that's good; if not, too bad."

For me, yes, I'll follow the law when I must do so and when the law is clear. I'll follow the law regardless of my personal views of the results, even if it is an unjust one. But where the law is not quite clear, or in the process of change, I'll look to the precedents and legal reasons that can support a result which I think is just, even if somewhat contrary to existing law. This philosophy often can put me at odds with my colleagues, but not always. My personal creed is: "Let justice be done."

In the Woosley case, the existing law needed to bend 180 degrees to do justice. We did it. That result becomes vividly illustrated in the opinions in the case of *Robert Michael Woosley v. United States,* decided in en banc (that is, by the full court) on April 24, 1973. I was very pleased and proud to write the decision.

Like Vaughn, the defendant Robert Woosley was a conscientious objector, but unlike Vaughan, Woosley sought to be classified as a minister in the Jehovah's Witness religion. That classification would exempt Woosley from both combatant and noncombatant service in the military. However, under the existing law, if Woosley had received a conscientious objector classification, he could be directed to do certain public service. To Woosley, this was contrary to his religious beliefs and his view against war. Nothing that would help the military effort would he do.

At the time the case came before us, Woosley was nineteen years of age, he was married and he and his wife were expecting a child within two months of his sentence, and he had been steadily employed. Because Woosley did not qualify for a ministerial exemption from the military draft and never sought to be classified as a conscientious objector, he was ordered to report for induction into the military. He refused.

Woosley sought a rehearing en banc and I supported him in that view. Pending the vote, Woosley's situation got worse. His wife suffered fatal injuries in an automobile accident when en route to visit him at the penitentiary. The couple had a small child. The majority of judges voted for an en banc hearing and to immediately release Woosley from prison.

The issue on appeal related to the sentence. At that time, a sentence by a district judge could not be reviewed or reversed on appeal with few exceptions. As the opinion's author, writing for the majority (five to four) of the en banc court, I said in part:

> The district court did not resort to appropriate standards in imposing sentence but utilized a "mechanical" and automatic approach in giving him a maximum prison sentence, as evidenced by the sentencing judge's similar treatment of all selective service violators who refused induction regardless of the circumstances of the violation or of the violator.
>
> We believe that we have the power to examine and review a sentence if it is shown to have been imposed on a mechanical basis.

I have always opposed harsh prison sentences for nonviolent criminals. The Woosley case stands as an early example.

Woosley came up on appeal at a time (1973) when the question of appellate review of sentences was a matter of discussion in the judiciary and not otherwise. One of the things in the back of my mind during this whole episode was a conversation I had had with then Chief Justice Warren Burger a few years earlier when I attended an appellate judges' course at New York University in New York City in the summer of 1969.

The new chief justice and I discussed sentencing on one occasion and I expressed the view that perhaps there should be appellate review of sentencing. He looked at me and said, "No way. Appellate judges don't know anything about sentencing."[10]

— CHAPTER 25 —

Reserve Mining — Jobs v. Environment

This chapter deals with one of the most important environmental litigation cases that arose in the 1970s. It concerns the pollution of one of the Great Lakes of our country — Lake Superior. The federal government charged that Reserve Mining Company was polluting Lake Superior and therefore the site should be closed down. A case called *Reserve Mining Co. v. United States* (1974) raised the matters.

This was a complicated case in its testimony of scientific witnesses and related to matters on the very periphery or cutting edge of science. It proved to be a very difficult case to analyze under the law for judges and we did the best we could. I might say that time has proved the correctness of our analysis and our decisions. But let us go back to the beginning with my court.

In April of 1974, members of the court were in Springfield, Missouri, attending a sentencing institute. Sometime during that day, Chief Judge M. Charles Matthes approached me and said, "Myron, there is a very important case from Judge Miles Lord coming up today. Judge Lord just closed up the Reserve Mining Company facility in Minnesota and Reserve Mining Company is asking that his order be stayed. It is an emergency and they are coming to Springfield today toward evening to represent their motion to stay Miles Lord's closing of the plant. I am appointing you to preside over the panel of Judge Ross and Judge Webster."

My mind went wheeeew!

I talked to Ross and Webster about the emergency situation and we decided to set up a temporary courtroom right in one of the hotel rooms. The panel, after hearing arguments and reviewing the various papers filed by the parties, agreed that it wouldn't immediately harm the public to allow Reserve Mining's continued operations for a short period of time until we learned more about the case.

This case reminded me of my background. I had lived in mining towns, Gilbert and Eveleth, and I remembered many occasions when the mines had closed for strikes, lack of business or other reasons. I remember the hardship to those who had worked in the mines. Parents of my friends could no longer rely on a regular paycheck. The parents of one of my best friends were on the verge of poverty when the mines closed.

My dad was a merchant and his customers could not pay their bills unless the miners worked. He sold merchandise on credit. My father never turned down a miner/customer, whether he was working or not, from charging merchandise. It took a long time for some of those customers to pay their bills, but they did. My father was cognizant of the hardships of those who worked in the mines and who would be unemployed during the cessation of mining operations.

I recognized the hardship to the people who worked for Reserve Mining in Silver Bay, where approximately thirty-three hundred people were employed in mining operations. The record shows that the work of every miner supported anywhere from five to seven other people indirectly who relied on mining operations. Thus, fifteen thousand to seventeen thousand people would be immediately affected by this shutdown.

I know we were faced with a very important issue. Should we keep the mines open or was there a health hazard? We recognized our responsibility as judges to remove health hazards from our environment. This was certainly one of the most important early environmental cases that had come into the federal courts. In many ways, the issue put in conflict jobs and the environment.

After argument, I assigned the case to myself and I immediately began drafting a proposed opinion. For a good long period of time, I did no work on any other case but Reserve Mining.

The hearing on whether or not to stay the injunction related to only a preliminary matter. The case had not been resolved. The difficulties in the case were such that I felt, as the author, I should say something about settlement. I suggested the parties attempt to settle the lawsuit.

In our opinion, we stayed the injunction to keep Reserve Mining open subject to good faith preparation and implementation of an acceptable plan by Reserve Mining to reduce the emission of tailings of its plant operations into the air and to take steps to discharge the tailings on land. With that, we remanded the case to the federal district court.

The merits of the case remained. On the merits, we heard the case en banc with all the judges from the Eighth Circuit who were not otherwise disqualified from sitting on this case. The opinion took up more than one-hundred double-spaced, typewritten pages. We essentially stated that Reserve must do something immediately to curb the emissions of taconite tailings into the air, but the company should be given a turnaround time to quit polluting Lake Superior.

In a *Minnesota Law Review* (Dec. 1998) article titled "The Legacy of Reserve Mining Company," Professor Daniel A. Farber, then of the University of Minnesota Law School, points out the importance of the Reserve Mining case in environmental law. He wrote, in part:

> In *Reserve Mining Co. v. EPA*, the federal courts first confronted one of the central dilemmas of environmental law. Often, the magnitude or very existence of a threat to public health or the environment is shrouded in scientific uncertainty. In the face of this uncertainty, how much of a burden should society be willing to bear to eliminate the risk? Judge Bright's answer to this question on behalf of the Eighth Circuit has become a lodestar for later judges and scholars ...
>
> Judge Bright's answer to this knotty question was that an immediate shut-down was too draconian, but that the company could not be allowed to continue indefinitely to place the public's health at risk. Hence, the company was ordered to make the conversion to land disposal expeditiously and to implement new air pollution controls. In reaching this conclusion, Judge Bright's opinion combined sensitivity to environmental values with a sense of proportion about the economic burdens of regulation.
>
> In my own view, this combination of sensitivity to environmental risks with realism about economic costs best fulfills our profound national commitment to the environment.

> Although we have learned more about environmental law and policy since Judge Bright's opinion in Reserve Mining, we have done well to follow down the path he opened in 1975. It has been said that hard cases make bad law. This is sometimes true; but as Reserve Mining illustrates, what is sometimes true instead is that a hard case can make for a pioneering judicial opinion.[11]

It has now been more than thirty-eight years since the principle Reserve Mining opinion was filed. These years have proved the correctness of the court's views that the discharge of tailings into the waters of Lake Superior had not caused any increase in cancer by persons who ingested this water. Nor has there been any increase in cancer that is known by persons in the Silver Bay area who may have breathed the air from the emissions from the taconite plant.

I think my background of having lived on the Iron Range of Minnesota and understanding the travails of people who worked in the iron mines helped in my understanding of some of the issues in this case. But did it influence my opinion? That is difficult to say. However, my sympathies were with the miners and my task focused on two issues — saving jobs and at the same time protecting the environment.[12]

— CHAPTER 26 —

Helm Case:
Judiciary Anarchy — Make the Most of It!

As a federal judge, I am required to follow precedents (statements of the law in similar cases) of the United States Supreme Court and federal circuit courts, including especially the circuit in which I am sitting. If a judge does not recognize and apply the precedent from his court in prior opinions or from the Supreme Court, in the words of the former Chief Justice Warren Burger and some of his colleagues, that judge could be deemed "a judicial anarchist." As I have said before, as a judge, I need to do justice, but I must also rely on the law to support my decision. That principle faced a great test with me in 1982.

In *Helm v. Solem* (1982), one may very well have described my opinion in the habeas case of Jerry Helm as a judicial anarchist. But let's look at the case from the way it developed from my perspective.

Helm v. Solem was an appeal from the denial of a habeas corpus petition by Jerry Helm against his prison superintendent in South Dakota. Helm was a thirty-six-year-old South Dakota resident and a confirmed alcoholic. Prior to the incident case, he had served about fifteen years in various prisons and penitentiaries in South Dakota, mostly for crimes that he had committed while he was inebriated.

The brief facts were that Helm had been convicted of a seventh nonviolent felony in South Dakota. He had issued a no-account check for about one hundred dollars. The district court judge looked at him and said you are, essentially, "no good." There is no rehabilitation for you. I am sentencing you as a habitual offender and you will serve the rest of your life in prison. Thus, for a rather minor crime, a nonviolent felony, the South Dakota trial judge sentenced Helm to life imprisonment without parole.

As I mentioned, this was his seventh nonviolent felony. Here and in past events, Helm would get drunk and either steal a little money or write a no-account check, and be prosecuted. He had been convicted for six prior felonies. He failed to get any relief in appealing to the South Dakota courts. He now came to the federal courts claiming the sentence was "cruel and unusual," violating the United States Constitution. In prior cases before the U.S. Supreme Court, the Court denied relief to persons convicted of nonviolent felonies (drug distributions and thefts) who received heavy prison sentences, including life imprisonment but with the possibility of parole, in the state courts.

A question in my mind: Here is a person that gets life imprisonment for a very minor crime and this court is to wipe off his application to this court for some relief with a brush saying, in effect, "This case is not worth an oral argument."

We granted Helm relief in our 1982 opinion. We concluded our opinion with the following:

> Helm could have received a life sentence without parole for his offense in only one other state, Nevada. Other states either did not authorize such a drastic sanction for habitual offenders, or require at least one prior felony conviction for a violent crime as a prerequisite to a sentence of life imprisonment without parole. Because Helm had no prior convictions for violent crimes ... he contends that life imprisonment without parole is grossly disproportionate to the severity of his offense. Based on our comparison of the laws of the other states, we agree.

Indeed, the state of South Dakota asked the Supreme Court for a review of our action. Wonder of all wonders, the Supreme Court affirmed our decision. I say that as a "wonder" the review was granted because the Supreme Court's cases seemed to call for a different decision. My opinion might be labeled "judicial anarchy."

Was I pleased to receive that opinion? I can say an enthusiastic yes and a surprised yes. Indeed, I was so pleased, I took it upon myself to write the author, Justice Powell, a letter which essentially said, "Thank you

Justice Powell for your fine opinion." His response to my letter had the following, "I understand your interest in *Solem v. Helm*. I thought you wrote a fine opinion and — as you can see — the reasoning of our opinions was substantially similar."

The difference between Helm as a prisoner and another case decided by the Supreme Court is that Helm's sentence was without the possibility of parole. That distinction in *Helm v. Solem* (8th Circuit) and the same case as *Solem v. Helm* in the Supreme Court amounted to a distinction with a difference. From that time on, Justice Powell and I became friends. I met him personally and we visited with each other on occasions.

The controversy reminded me of an earlier discussion of the function of a judge: (a) to do justice (according to Fritzie) or (b) to follow the law (according to Judge Richard S. Arnold) or (c) somewhere in between (according to me). We found a way to do justice within the law, although, as I mentioned, it was quite close to what others might call judicial anarchy. I have no doubt that with most judges on the appeals courts, Helm would have received no relief. The Supreme Court of South Dakota denied him relief. A person in the place of Helm would still be languishing, maybe even rotting, in prison. We got him out and that was a successful end.

In June 2010, the Supreme Court decided *Graham v. Florida*. The opinion, written by Justice Kennedy, relied on *Helm v. Solem* to reach a decision. Helm to some extent, got a heartbeat and a new life.

Graham followed *Helm* by some twenty-six years. After reading the Graham case, I wrote to the author, Justice Kennedy, and the other justice in the majority. I did get some interesting responses. Justice Kennedy wrote to thank me for being a devoted student of Supreme Court jurisprudence and of the law. He said, "It is good to know that there are members of the judiciary who care, who are so meticulous and thoughtful."

A note from Justice Sonia Sotomayor said, "It is wonderful for both of us to be part of history in such special ways."

Justice Sam Alito Jr., who dissented in the Graham case, commented that the information I provided "was intriguing."

Sotomayor's observation about us being part of history raises an interesting point: Yes, Supreme Court justices make history in the opinions of that court. But so do other judges, particularly judges in the federal courts whose decisions are reviewed by the country's highest court. To that extent, I've participated in making history, at least judicial history.

The lesson of *Solem, Graham,* and other similar cases, is that if a judge believes justice has not been done in a case, particularly a criminal case, it is not enough to just look basically at the precedents (other cases) without considering the underlying features of the cases decided compared against the case before the court at that time.

There were special features in Solem that persuaded our court and the author (me) to skirt precedent and decide in favor of the prisoner, Helm. The situation was similar in the Graham case. What will happen in the future? Time will tell.

What is the lesson of *Helm*? An imaginative judge seeking to do justice in a case even when precedent seems against a proper result must and should find a way to do justice within the law. Again my aversion to heavy unjustified prison sentences played a role in my decision-making.[13]

— CHAPTER 27 —

Green v. McDonnell Douglas: Not Any Old Excuse Will Do — a Seminal Case

After I became a federal judge in 1968, the first scheduled session fell in mid-September. Prior to the court's meeting, I enjoyed a dinner with Judge Gerald (Jerry) Heaney, who had been appointed to the U.S. Court of Appeals a year before me.

Jerry said to me, "Myron, this country cannot exist as a segregated society, as we now have it." He devoted his life's work, in many ways, to correcting that ill in our society as did I. One of the important cases in which I participated was *Green v. McDonnell Douglas* (1972), which made a big change in the way the courts looked at employment discrimination, in particular employment discrimination that was covert or hidden. Very seldom do employers admit that a black person or a woman was not hired because of his or her race or sex. But things were, as one would say, cooking at that time.

Percy Green was a civil rights activist; some might characterize him as a civil rights troublemaker. His background with McDonnell Douglas was as follows: In 1956, McDonnell Douglas employed Green as a mechanic. He remained with the company continuously, except for twenty-one months of honorable military service, until he was laid off on August 28, 1964. His layoff came because of a lack of work and without any discriminatory motive. Nevertheless, Green, a longtime activist in the movement to obtain equal rights for black citizens, vigorously protested his discharge as racially motivated. His protests were without any success.

The business cycle changed and on July 25, 1965, McDonnell Douglas ran an advertisement in the St. Louis newspapers seeking qualified electrical mechanics. The next day, Green applied. Although he was well-qualified, McDonnell Douglas refused to hire him. Green filed a formal complaint with the Equal Employment Opportunity Commission, claiming he had not been hired because of his race and because of his persistent involvement in the civil rights movement. Both of these contentions, if proved, would fall within the contours of the new Civil Rights Act.

McDonnell Douglas, of course, rested its whole case on its assertion that Green had been a troublemaker. Green had participated in two events that were disruptive to the interests of the employer. One was a stall-in, where he and others had blocked the roads into the McDonnell Douglas plant, making it difficult for the employees to get there for a morning shift. That effort delayed and impeded employees in their work and was against the interest of McDonnell Douglas. They contended that this was a good enough reason for not hiring a troublemaker.

Secondly, McDonnell Douglas asserted that Green had participated in what was called the lock-in, where civil rights activists had chained the doors of the McDonnell Douglas offices in downtown St. Louis.

I was positive that Green should have the opportunity to have his Title VII case fairly tried in the district court on issues that related to discrimination.

The issue was not *overt* discrimination. McDonnell Douglas claimed that it did not discriminate in its employment policies. The issue for determination was what test should be applied when it is claimed that the employer was guilty of covert or hidden discrimination in its employment decisions. The cases in the federal courts had not resolved that issue and neither had the U. S. Supreme Court.

In my initial opinion, I wrote that Green, as a black person, a member of the minority race and covered by Title VII, was certainly conceded to be qualified for the job. When he did not get the position, it was the employer's obligation to show that its reasons for denying employment were job related. Moreover, I had also said that in decisions relating to employment practices, those decisions based on subjective rather than objective criteria would carry little weight in rebutting the charges of discrimination. McDonnell Douglas asked for a rehearing by the full court, then eight judges. Its request was supported by a strong dissent to my opinion. Judge Donald P. Lay had agreed with my opinion. Judge Harvey Johnsen wrote a very critical dissent. A rehearing en banc was probable.

I knew that the *Green v. McDonnell Douglas* opinion that I had written was on a precipice. To get a rehearing en banc (by full court), the petition by the McDonnell Douglas Corporation needed five votes (a majority of the eight judges then on the court). I knew three judges would vote against such a rehearing (Lay, Heaney and Bright) and four judges would vote for a rehearing. The swing person or vote was from Judge Donald Ross of Omaha, Nebraska. If Ross would vote with me making a tie four-to-four vote, there would not be a rehearing and we would accomplish some good in the law regarding the civil rights movement relating to nondiscriminatory employment practices.

I talked to Judge Ross by telephone, "Don, why don't you write out what you want me to say in my opinion and I will do so and satisfy you?"

He said, "Myron, I will do so." He did send me a new part of the opinion and I then modified my opinion. The revised portion essentially written by Judge Ross said:

> "... and when a black man demonstrates that he possesses the qualifications to fill a job opening and that he was denied the job which continues to remain open, we think he presents a prima facie case of racial discrimination. However, an applicant's past participation in unlawful conduct directed at his prospective employer might indicate the applicant's lack of a responsible attitude toward performing work for that employer.
>
> Of the several civil rights protests which Green directed against McDonnell, the employer selected two, the "lock-in and the "stall-in," as reasons for its refusal to hire Green. Green should be given the opportunity to show that these reasons offered by the Company were pretextual, or otherwise show the presence of racially discriminatory hiring practices by McDonnell which affected its decision.
>
> The district court did not use appropriate standards in determining whether McDonnell's refusal to hire Green was racially motivated. On remand, both parties will have the

opportunity to present evidence on this matter. (Footnote omitted).

The request for a rehearing en banc was denied. McDonnell Douglas petitioned for a writ of certiorari to the Supreme Court. In an opinion in which all justices joined, the Court essentially adopted the test for covert discrimination from the prior panel opinion with the changes requested by Judge Ross. Here's the statement of the rule:

> The complainant in a Title VII trial must carry the initial burden under the statute of establishing a prima facie case of racial discrimination. This may be done by showing (i) that he belongs to a racial minority; (ii) that he applied and was qualified for a job for which the employer was seeking applicants; (iii) that, despite his qualifications, he was rejected; and (iv) that, after his rejection, the position remained open and the employer continued to seek applicants from persons of complainant's qualifications.

The Court then added:

> The burden then must shift to the employer to articulate some legitimate, nondiscriminatory reason for the employee's rejection. Such non-discriminate reason meets the prima facie case and then in order to succeed the complainant must show by competent evidence that the presumptively valid reasons for his rejection were in fact a cover up for a racially discriminatory decision or to put it in other words, that the reasons were pretextual.

That was the rule and the Supreme Court did remand this case for further proceedings. The only real criticism of the Eighth Circuit opinion was that the Eighth Circuit underestimated the company's rebuttal weight to be given to the evidence from Green's admission that he had taken part in the stall-in, which was designed to tie up access and egress from petitioner's plant at a peak traffic hour.

The only issue with meaning on remand to the Eighth Circuit would be that Green would have the opportunity to show that this reason was pretextual and therefore would not absolve the employer.

Green v. McDonnell Douglas and the rule enunciated there became one of the most important cases helpful in eradicating unlawful prejudice as a barrier to employment of men or women. As of April 2013, the Supreme Court case has been referenced 132,493 times by courts throughout the country. It is the test that is not only adopted for employment discrimination under Title VII but, additionally, with slight variation, the test has applied to improper employment discrimination under federal law including sex and disability.

This case is one of the most important cases in creating a nonsegregated society in this country. On television you see men and women of all colors, of all races on the screen. We who have lived through the past half century know that our society has changed dramatically and that people of both genders and all races are equals in employment. *Green v. McDonnell Douglas* was a harbinger of other cases that said to employers: "You shall not discriminate in employment because of prejudice with individual race, color, religion, gender or national origin."

I especially dedicate this chapter to my good friend, Judge Ross. I tried to give him ample credit for his contribution to *Green v. McDonnell Douglas* when I spoke at the unveiling of his portrait upon his taking senior status as a judge of the U.S. Court of Appeals for the Eighth Circuit on October 30, 1987, in the U. S. Courthouse in Omaha: Justice Powell wrote the opinion for the U.S. Supreme Court, but the idea and the basic text came from my "buddy" Ross. In fact, if I had used all Ross' language, the Powell standards precisely equaled the views of Ross.

At the portrait unveiling ceremony for Judge Ross, his response to me was:

> Now, Judge Bright has been my friend, as he said, for about seventeen years and he has never stopped trying to turn me into a liberal judge, and when he is unable to convince me that way in court, he makes speeches in which he tells people how liberal I am. (Laughter) At one point, he even tried to convert me to Judaism (laughter), but as he demonstrated today, his sense of humor and ability to speak have been appreciated by all of us, both off and on the bench.

Regardless of political or judicial philosophy, most federal judges strongly enforce antidiscrimination laws. Having known of and felt unfair discrimination myself, I have a concern that I should do all that I can do to limit or eradicate wrongful discrimination under law.[14]

— CHAPTER 28 —

Unfinished Business — Sentencing Appeals

Sentencing guidelines in the United States courts greatly affected my most recent extensive dissent of *Deegan v. United States* (2010).

In my senior years as a United States circuit judge, I consider unfinished business my views on sentencing guidelines during the guideline mandatory period of 1987 until that became nonbinding in January 2005. I wrote many dissenting opinions in guideline sentencing appeals. Let me discuss my disagreements with majority opinions written by my judicial colleagues.

First, in cases where there exists no precedential or earlier opinion or opinions in the court in which I sit or by the U.S. Supreme Court, I show my disagreement with the decision of the panel majority (two judges in a three-judge panel) by authoring a dissent.

In addition, I may sit on an en banc court (whole court), consisting of the active judges (currently eleven), to reconsider the panel majority opinion and any dissent therein. By an order of the en banc court, the panel decision under review will usually be vacated (set aside). A senior judge, such as I, can elect to sit on the en banc court if that senior judge was on the original three-judge panel.

My disagreement with a panel majority opinion or an en banc court majority opinion can be written as a dissent or separate concurrence on one or more issues. When I write a separate concurrence, I am agreeing with the end result in the majority decision but express some disagreement with the reasoning in that opinion. In a dissent, I disagree with the result.

As an appellate judge, I am obligated to follow the law or factual determinations applying the law in prior cases decided by the court — either a panel opinion or an en banc opinion or a Supreme Court ruling. My separate opinion says the majority is wrong. But, in stating a separate view, I in no way denigrate my colleagues who are in the majority. In court cases, there can be and often are honest disagreements among judges about the construction of the facts and the proper application of the law.

Who is right? Well, the majority rules. Does that mean I can be out of step with the majority in that case? Yes! Differences do and can exist between and among judges concerning the facts and/or application of law in a case. I wrote about those differences in an article "Getting There. Do Philosophy and Oral Argument Influence Decisions?" This article, published in the *American Bar Association Journal* in 1991, asserts that the philosophy of judges influences their decision-making. In that article, I asserted, in essence, that judges tend to look at the facts of a case through their own rose-colored glasses. In other words, personal views influence judicial decision-making.

Lawyers long have known that the outcome of an appeal raising a novel or controversial question of law often turns on the judge or judges deciding the case. For example, it is no secret that a difficult issue posed to the U.S. Supreme Court often led to remarkably different analyses and outcomes by, say, Chief Justice William Rehnquist and Justice William Brennan.

But cases involving interpretation of the law are the exception, not the rule. Most judges subsist largely on a diet of cases requiring straightforward review of the factual record and application of those facts to settled legal principles.

What about these cases? Does the judge's philosophy play an important role? A survey I conducted at the Seventh National Appellate Practice Institute suggests that it does. In April 1990, lawyers from across the United States gathered in New Orleans at the institute, sponsored by the American Bar Association's Appellate Judges Conference and the National Institute, to sharpen their appellate skills. They briefed and argued the same case before three judges acting as a panel. Forty-five panel judges, mostly federal appeals court judges but some lawyers and state court judges, participated in the institute.

The facts of the case presented an arrest by police of two African Americans.

To examine the extent to which judicial philosophy and oral argument may have influenced the judges' decisions, I prepared a questionnaire and submitted it to the forty-five faculty judges. It contained only three questions:

1. As to each of the two plaintiffs, would the judge have voted for affirmance or reversal of the district court's denial of the police motion for summary judgment on qualified immunity grounds?
2. Did the judge's view of the case change after oral argument?
3. In terms of judicial philosophy or viewpoint, which of the following Supreme Court justices did the judge feel most closely in tune with: Chief Justice Rehnquist, Justices Brennan, White, Marshall, Blackmun, Stevens, O'Connor, Scalia or Kennedy?

Thirty-one of forty-five institute judges responded.

In tabulating the results according to judicial philosophy, I rejected the terms "liberal," "moderate" and "conservative." Instead, the responses were grouped in terms of compatibility with the Warren Court, the Burger Court or the Rehnquist Court.

From the survey and from my experience serving as a federal judge then for the past twenty-two years, I offered these observations to lawyers: judicial philosophy or viewpoint can make a difference in the result, even in a fact-oriented case. Facts are in the eye of the beholder. Faculty judges identifying with the Warren and Burger Courts, on the one hand, tended to view the facts in a light sufficient to enable the civil-rights plaintiffs to proceed to trial. Faculty judges identifying with the Rehnquist Court, on the other hand, generally voted in favor of the police and for immediate dismissal.

I asked for comments on my article from two individuals. One was Circuit Judge Leonard I. Garth of the Third Circuit, a Nixon appointee who served as chairman of the ABA Committee for Appellate Practice for several years. He's a great judge, a friend and a person I admire. His comments disagreed with my views:

> My ultimate disposition was influenced only by the governing jurisprudence in the field, and not by what Judge Bright would call my judicial philosophy.

> In sum, I just do not believe that in a fact-sensitive, non-public interest case similar to the one that the institute considered, and similar in nature to most of the appeals we decide, the judicial philosophy of the judge has anything to do with the outcome. Rather, the outcome of that appeal is dictated, I think, by the judge's reasoned view of the case, guided by precedent, common sense and fairness.

Another view tended to agree with me. Andrew Frey, a prominent lawyer who frequently argues cases before the United States Supreme Court and other appeals courts, made these written comments:

> The fate of an appeal is often foreordained by its inherent merits (or lack thereof) no matter which judges hear it, while the outcome of at least some others is predetermined by the identity of the judges and is unlikely to be influenced by the best of advocates. But there remains a significant body of appeals in which open-minded (or even predisposed) judges could reasonably go either way.
>
> I happen to view myself as being quite non-ideological in my outlook toward most legal issues. In this case, my vote to affirm was quite unshakable and, I think, beyond being changed by even the most persuasive advocate. Nevertheless, nearly half of those responding to Judge Bright's survey would have reversed at least in part.
>
> This tells us not only about the potential influence of personal philosophy on the votes of the most well-intentioned judges, but also that we must be cautious in making predictions about the outcome of any case simply on the basis of our own assessment of the issues.

In a general way, I agree with Frey. Many appealed cases are pre-ordained in result regardless of a judge's philosophy, but others, which have merit to either side, can be influenced in the decision by a judge's philosophy. While I may disagree with judicial colleagues, I do not undertake to say that I am right and he or she, as a judge, is wrong. Individuals can and do have real and honest differences of opinion. Thus, I suggest the reader of my opinions may agree or disagree with what I say.

In the next chapters, I outline my disagreements with the prison sentences imposed in several cases applying federal sentencing guidelines.

Further, I write of my disagreement with guideline sentencing, even as discretionary, as it affects Native Americans living on reservations generally. Also, I write about a specific case of a North Dakota Native American young woman, Dana Deegan, who is serving a long prison sentence imposed in the federal courts while a white woman charged for a similar crime committed at about the same time received a lenient sentence, no jail time, in a state court of North Dakota. That unequal treatment concerned me greatly. I wrote a sixty-five-page dissent in the Deegan case, which I discuss later.

— CHAPTER 29 —

My Sentencing Philosophy

During my time in the military service, I defended soldiers charged with crimes under military law. Some of the charges appeared not of great import, including the following types of cases which come to mind: offending military law by urinating in a public place; violating military orders not to leave the troopship when docked in Melbourne, Australia; committing homosexual sex on a military base; using the company commander's military vehicle without permission; etc. None of the violations seemed serious. I successfully defended each of these cases.

As a lawyer, I defended only a very few clients in criminal cases. I did handle a few misdemeanor cases in county court: shooting big game (a moose) where there is no season for moose, a driving-while-intoxicated charge, and a political offense of improperly validating a voter's name on an application for an absentee ballot when the violator, a notary public, did not witness the signing of the application. None of these may seem very serious transgressions of the law, but the charges were serious for the defendants. I won or attained a good result in each case.

I did try a felony case in federal court: A young man had written false insurance policies and received monetary commissions on those policies from his employer. The federal government charged the young man with obtaining money by fraud. The jury rejected my defense that the employer's procedures and training contributed to the fraud. The trial judge, Ronald N. Davies of Fargo, was a judge with a heart; sentencing laws then were quite humane and, in my view, reasonable. The jury found the defendant guilty of fraud against his employer.

Under the existing laws, Judge Davies imposed a deferred prison sentence. With good behavior for a substantial period of time, such an offender could be relieved of the effects of the conviction. This young man subsequently completed his education, got married, held a steady job and conducted himself as a good citizen. His conviction became wiped out under the deferred sentence laws. Those federal provisions do not now exist.

In my years as a federal judge, I have examined many appeals in criminal cases. From 1968 to 1987, before the advent of the sentencing guidelines, very few of the criminal cases in which I participated included the length of prison sentence as an issue on appeal. The sentencing judge's determination was ordinarily not subject to appellate review. However, I did observe the disparity of sentences imposed for similar crimes by various district judges.

As covered in a previous chapter, I did hear and decide one memorable sentencing case during the military draft for the Vietnam War. The Eighth Circuit, in an opinion that I wrote in the *Vaughn v. United States* case, ruled that the mandatory maximum five-year prison sentence for persons convicted of refusing to enter military service under the draft laws could be reversed. The reversal rested on the basis that the district judges in those cases could not automatically impose the five-year maximum sentence on all violators.

I served on the Probation Committee of the Judicial Conference of the United States during the years 1977-1983. We learned about problems in criminal sentencing; among other things, taught judges principles of proper sentencing in sentencing seminars held at various places in the United States; visited federal prisons; and talked with prison administrators and persons engaged in the operation of prisons as well as with prisoners themselves.

This was a real learning experience and an eye opener. I came to the belief that many persons in jail could be rehabilitated with proper training. I also recognized that some should be incarcerated for long periods of time to protect the public. The system then in existence to 1987 had its flaws. However, in my view, the sentencing procedures under the mandatory guidelines beginning in 1987 were a disaster. Since the Booker case in 2005, the guidelines have become advisory and the system has improved. However, the differing philosophies of district judges play a role in unequal sentencing of persons found guilty of federal crimes where there exist little differences among defendants. So let's talk about the federal sentencing guidelines.

In *O'Meara v. Kost* (1990), I essentially said in dissent that the Kost sentence is a bizarre one, almost double that of his co-conspirator O'Meara. Kost was a young man facing his first federal sentence. O'Meara was a more experienced criminal. O'Meara knew what to say — admit everything and get a low guidelines sentence.

Kost tried to protect O'Meara but the judge did not believe his story. Result: The bad guy and more experienced criminal gets less time than the new person on the block.

The Kost case proved to be only the beginning of a long string of opinions by Myron, dissents or separate concurrences in which I criticized sentencing under the guidelines as often unfair, improper and wrong, noting, among other things, that guideline sentences took humanity out of sentencing as it was computed by the numbers; many sentences, often excessive in length, ignored differences in the persons committing crimes. Often the least criminally responsible person in a conspiracy got a heavier sentence than the leaders; the heavy sentences for drug cases represented the war on drugs that the government continues to lose but still incarcerates people for unnecessary long periods of time.

I could write another book about unfair guideline sentences, but instead I authored scores of opinions calling guideline sentencing unreasonable and part of a topsy-turvy world of sentencing. I said in one critical opinion: "Is anyone out there listening?"

Fortunately, as I have said, the Supreme Court of the United States stepped in and decided the *United States v. Booker* case in 2005 which held the guidelines as advisory instead of mandatory. Then, in succeeding cases, the court emphasized that discretion in sentencing rested with the district judge, the sentencing judge, and not the reviewing court.

This change to advisory guidelines has been a good one with exceptions. Too many U.S. district judges personally like the guidelines and still sentence by them as though the guidelines are good guides and should be followed. In that procedure, the judge relies on probation officers to compute the guidelines applicable; the judge then applies the guideline sentence. In effect, probation officers do the sentencing.

In this process, the sentencing judge ignores the admonition of Congress that "the court shall impose a sentence sufficient, but not greater than necessary, to comply with the purposes [related to sentencing]."

I summarized my overall views about guideline sentencing in a concurring opinion I authored in the case of *United States v. Hiveley* (1995). I wrote that "unwise sentencing policies which put men and women in prison for years, not only ruin lives ... but also drain the American taxpayers. It is time to call a halt to the unnecessary and expensive cost of putting people in prison for a long time based on the mistaken notion that such an effort will win *The War on Drugs*."

I added, "The public needs to know that unnecessary, harsh and unreasonable drug sentences serve to waste billions of dollars without doing much good for society." I also said, "We have an unreasonable system."

After the *Booker* opinion by the Supreme Court in 2005, as well as some others later relating to sentencing following the Booker case, I wrote to my good friend on the court, Justice Ruth Bader Ginsburg, commending those decisions. I am gratified by her reply in which she said that "a lot of the credit belongs to you for advocating the right approach so forcibly and persistently."

I now say to Congress: Get rid of sentencing guidelines as they now exist. It's time to reform the system. Indeed, a new day may be dawning in federal sentencing. On August 12, 2013, in a speech at the annual meeting of the American Bar Association House of Delegates, U.S. Attorney General Eric H. Holder Jr. called for a different approach on criminal sentencing in the federal courts.[15]

He cited "unwarranted disparities" in a criminal justice system that is "in too many respects broken."

Concerning the so-called war on drugs, Holder said we need to ensure that incarceration is used to punish, deter and rehabilitate — not merely to warehouse and forget. Most importantly, he summarized the current imprisonment of people as being clear "that too many Americans go to too many prisons for far too long, and for no truly good law enforcement reason."

Holder announced a new federal policy for federal prosecutors stating that some issues should be handled at the state or local level, and that the U. S. attorney community should develop specific, locally tailored guidelines for determining when federal charges should be filed and when they should not.

He also addressed the high cost of improper incarceration, stating that widespread incarceration at the federal, state and local levels is both ineffective and unsustainable, noting that it imposes a significant economic burden — totaling $80 billion in 2010 alone — and it comes with human and moral costs that are impossible to calculate.

Holder focused on rethinking the notion of mandatory minimum sentences in general but in particular for drug-related crimes. He would make the Justice Department's charging policies better suited than "draconian mandatory minimum sentences."

To this speech and its reflection of a changed view about federal sentencing, I say: "Hurrah!" And, "it's about time!"

In response, on August 27, 2013, I wrote to the attorney general, stating that his speech echoed many of the same sentiments I have expressed in opinions over the past twenty-plus years.

One of my first cases (O'Meara) reviewing a sentence after the guidelines were implemented in 1987 related to an experienced drug criminal who was sentenced to less jail time than his young neophyte counterpart. This case, I advised Holder, "Opens the window on the sometimes bizarre and topsy-turvy world of sentencing under the Guidelines."[16]

In another notable case (Hiveley) I wrote about the paradigm of what judges often see in the sentencing of drug law offenders. In this case, the sentences are excessively long but required by the mandatory minimum sentencing pro-visions and the overlaying requirements of the federal sentencing guidelines. I indicated that these unwise sentencing policies which put men and women in prison for years not only ruin lives of prisoners and often their family members, but also drain the American taxpayers of funds which can be measured in billions of dollars. In these times, I wrote, the government, Congress and the president see the need to make drastic cuts in the federal budget, including budget cuts which already affect the poor, the disadvantaged and the elderly.

> This is the time to call a halt to the unnecessary and expensive cost of putting people in prison for a long time based on the mistaken notion that such an effort will win "The War on Drugs." If it is a war, society seems not to be winning, but losing. We must turn to other methods of deterring drug distribution and use. Long sentences do not work ... .[17]

In still another concurring opinion, *United States v. England*,[18] I again emphasized that with respect to our current sentencing policies, it is time for re-evaluation and change. As these and many other of my opinions highlight, I have been a consistent critic of the guidelines, particularly as they relate to sentencing for nonviolent drug offenses.

In my letter, I also commented on Attorney General Holder's observations of disparity in sentencing. He mentioned differences in sentences between black males (harsh) and white males (less harsh). I referred to another sentencing disparity that is often overlooked and is particularly acute in the Dakotas, sentencing of American Indians.

I noted that when a Native American is convicted of one of the major crimes enumerated in 18 U.S.C. § 1153 (the Major Crimes Act) for an act he or she commits on a reservation that is subject to federal jurisdiction, he or she is sentenced under the federal guidelines. But others (predominantly white persons) committing similar crimes off the reservation are subject to state laws. These laws in many states carry significantly shorter sentences, often with options for probation and parole. The result is that Native American offenders are often subject to disproportionately harsh sentences simply because of their race and living on a reservation. That is simply wrong, and it needs to be addressed and corrected.

I also called attention to lengthy incarcerations of nonviolent criminals. Holder had indicated that approximately half of the 219,000 federal prisoners currently behind bars are guilty of drug-related crimes. A substantial percentage of them are nonviolent offenders.[19] Overall, nonviolent offenders constitute over sixty percent of the nation's prison and jail population, and they account for twenty-five percent of all offenders behind bars. Our country currently spends more than $75 billion per year on corrections. Reducing the number of nonviolent offenders in our prisons and jails by half would save our nation $16.9 billion per year. It would save the federal government $2.1 billion per year."[20]

I advised the attorney general that some method should be implemented to afford nonviolent drug offenders early relief. A possible procedure would be executive clemency — specifically, commutation of sentences.

Let us hope for early implementation of the changes outlined by Attorney General Holder.

— CHAPTER 30 —

Dana Deegan — Reservation Injustice

The use of guideline sentencing to impose an overly harsh sentence on a greatly oppressed Native American woman of fine character, Dana Deegan, who lived on the Fort Berthold Indian Reservation, is a case of injustice and represents unfinished business that needs to be addressed by people of North Dakota, Native Americans and all of us. That case demonstrates unequal justice to a Native American woman sentenced for a crime on the reservation to ten years in a federal prison, as compared to a young non-Indian woman who committed a similar crime at about the same time and was prosecuted in a North Dakota state court. The non-Indian woman received probation with no jail time.

I have never encountered a worse case of injustice between a non-Indian woman and a Native American woman. The majority judges viewed the circumstances through their own rose-colored glasses[21] to sustain the heavy and disparate sentence; I reviewed the sentence imposed by the sentencing judge through my own rose-colored glasses, strongly disagreed with the majority, and advocated reversing the district judge and vacating the sentence.

I stand by my dissent but recognize that the majority rules and, at this time, that opinion represents the state of the law regarding *United States v. Dana Deegan* (2010). However, I will focus on a matter not fully considered in the Deegan case and not brought to the attention of the U.S. Supreme Court in the petition and brief by the lawyers for the defendant. The Supreme Court did not accept the case for review. An issue of unequal justice remains.

Deegan is a member of the Three Affiliated Tribes in North Dakota. On October 20, 1998, she secretly gave birth to a baby boy in the bathroom of her home on the Fort Berthold Indian Reservation. The baby was alive and breathing when he was delivered. Deegan had kept her pregnancy hidden, and no other adult was present at the time of the delivery. Her three other minor children were in the home, but they were unaware of the birth.

Approximately two hours after delivering her son, Deegan fed, cleaned and dressed him, and then placed him in a basket. She then left the house with her other children, intentionally leaving the baby alone without food, water or a caregiver. Deegan did not return home for approximately two weeks. When she returned, she found the baby dead in the basket where she had left him. She put his remains in a suitcase, which she deposited in a rural ditch area near her residence.

The death of the baby at the hands of Ms. Deegan led the federal government, which had the sole right to prosecute crimes committed on an Indian reservation, to charge Ms. Deegan with second-degree murder.

Neonaticide, the killing of a newborn child on the first day of life, represents a crime practically unknown in the federal courts. Because neonaticide is a crime relating to family and domestic concerns, most of those cases arise in the state courts. Excluding the Deegan case, our research disclosed only one other reported federal case of neonaticide.[22]

Deegan, through her attorney, admitted guilt and thus was to be sentenced by a federal judge.

This was Ms. Deegan's only offense. The guidelines are said to apply to typical crimes under the applicable criminal law. The guidelines under federal law are not mandatory, only advisory. If a judge does not sentence under the guidelines, he or she should consider the nature of the crime, the background of the defendant and the interest of the public in levying a sentence that deters others from committing a similar crime. Educational or vocational training in prison for the defendant should also be considered. These are referred by the federal statute as "Section 3553a" factors in sentencing.

In the hearings on the sentence, the federal district judge (the sentencing judge) learned the nature of the crime, the reasons for Deegan's abandonment of the newborn — which was unexpected and delivered by

Deegan without any assistance — and much about Deegan's background leading up to this neonaticide crime.

The young woman's life is marked by a history of suffering extensive and cruel abuse for almost all of her then twenty-five years of life. First, from an alcoholic father who beat her on an almost daily basis and dominated every aspect of her life. Some of the beatings were so severe that her father kept her home from school to avoid reports to Child Protective Services on the Indian reservation. She was removed from her parents' house many times. She also experienced physical abuse in foster homes.

Her father was also, in a way, responsible indirectly for cruel sexual abuse. His drunken companions began abusing her sexually at the age of five and she was forced to participate in oral, vaginal and anal sex. She was tortured by one of the perpetrators who held her head under water several times to make her submissive and threatened her so she would not disclose the abuse. Finally, at age eleven, the sexual abuse ended when Deegan told her mother. Her father responded by beating her for being a "slut and allowing it to happen."

During her early years, Deegan spent much of her time caring for and otherwise trying to protect her other six younger siblings from abuse.

At age fifteen, Deegan began a relationship with Shannon Hale, the son of her foster parents. Hale continued the abuse and beat her so badly she had to be hospitalized. In the meantime, she bore four children fathered by Hale, including the infant victim in this case.

The record showed that after Deegan's third child was born, she became depressed. Hale was physically abusing her two or three times per week, forcing her to have sexual intercourse with him and refusing to care for their children. Two days before she delivered their third child, Hale choked her and threw her onto gravel, causing injuries that persisted for several months.

On October 20, 1998, alone in her mobile home with her three children, Deegan went into labor with her fourth child. She did not tell anyone and delivered the child herself. She reported not feeling anything physically from the labor and that she had assisted the infant to breathe when he was born.

Deegan was at her wits' end. She was in poverty. She didn't think she could care for her other three children. She said she was overwhelmed and oppressed and didn't want to live through any of it anymore. She didn't want to be there anymore as a spouse, as a mother or as a daughter. When asked why she left her child in the home alone, she replied:

> I couldn't take anymore. I couldn't handle it. I had everything on my shoulders. I couldn't even help myself. I had nobody to help me. I had no job, no nothing. I had all my babies to care for, a welfare mom. I had the feeling of being worthless. What could I do? I was overwhelmed and depressed. I didn't want to live through any of it anymore. I didn't want to be there anymore, as a spouse, as a mother as a daughter.

Because this crime related to one seldom heard in any federal court, the following comments by Dr. Philip Resnick, an expert physician in the area of medicine described below, were presented to the sentencing judge:

> Neonaticide is simply the killing of a newborn infant on the first day of life. It's actually a term that I coined in an article I wrote in 1969 where I was distinguishing that type of killing of a baby, which has very different characteristics, from the killing of a baby who is older or a child. And so neonaticide has universally been accepted now as a particular phenomenon when the baby is killed the first day of life.

Dr. Resnick's testimony was important in understanding Deegan's crime. Here's a summary: That crime of neonaticide most often reflects a mother who is in an overwhelming state of desperation at the time of the birth of her infant and usually lacks adequate resources to physically or mentally handle the situation. The birth of the child is often hidden.

There are two profiles for the crime of neonaticide. Dr. Resnick, who testified at the trial, made an extensive psychiatric examination of Deegan and concluded that she was suffering from a major depressive disorder at the time she abandoned her infant. He described two types of women who commit neonaticide. One type is a young woman, often unmarried, who cannot cope with the birth of an unwanted child and is very much afraid of offending her parents, particularly her mother. The other type would be a woman who has suffered great abuse throughout her life and cannot cope with the birth of an unwanted child.

The doctor testified regarding Deegan's background and noted that she did not have significant support from her family and community.

Deegan lived in a rural home, in a rural area of North Dakota and she lacked the financial resources to leave her abusive and troubled family life. She did not have outreach services for which she could have received assistance. Nor were there shelters for victims of domestic violence on the reservation.

At the time, North Dakota did not yet have a safe haven law whereby parents could bring a child for which they felt unable to provide care and leave that child at certain places. Individuals and institutions had consistently failed Deegan when she needed help.

At sentencing, the prosecutor, ignoring the special circumstances affecting Ms. Deegan in the neonaticide case, recommended a guideline sentence and said to the judge:

> The United States believes that the Sentencing Commission took into account these type of events, these type of crimes when it put together sentencing guidelines such as exist in the 1997 edition. Given that fact, Your Honor, we believe that a guideline sentence would effectively meet the requirements of Section 3553, all of those goals of sentencing.

The district court agreed with the prosecutor that the guidelines provide honesty in sentencing and are fair, and sentenced Deegan to the 121 months. The district judge said he took Dr. Resnick's testimony into account and had considered Deegan's harsh background but could not ignore that an innocent life had been taken.

Dr. Resnick's testimony indicated that in similar neonaticide cases in the courts of various states, the sentences seldom exceeded three years. Further, during the sentencing hearing, the counsel for Deegan advised the sentencing judge that in a neonaticide crime in North Dakota committed by a young woman not on an Indian reservation, the state imposed a sentence of probation.

I was one of the three federal judges hearing Deegan's appeal. The majority affirmed the sentence as not excessive and as imposed in accordance with proper procedures, *United States v. Deegan*, (2010). I wrote a sixty-five-page dissent asserting that the prosecutor and the sentencing judge did not know or realize that the guidelines did not cover the atypical homicide called neonaticide as committed by Deegan.

Talk about excessiveness. Here was Deegan, who, in her mental state, thought she needed to abandon her newborn to protect the lives of her three young daughters. She was shown to be a great mother. The goal of sentencing — of imposing a sentence not greater than necessary — was not met in this case.

In my dissent seeking reversal, I said that the sentence of over ten years lacked any basis in the guidelines. The guidelines were intended to apply to the ordinary crimes charged under the statute (in-the-ballpark crimes), not the unusual ones such as in this case. The prosecutor did not know and obviously had not checked into that aspect that could affect sentencing.

While it is true that state sentences are not usually taken into account in federal sentencing, here we had an entirely different situation: a similar crime committed in North Dakota but not on an Indian reservation is one in which no prison time at all is imposed on the defendant, while the same crime committed in federal court calls for ten years.

I said in one of my opinions that the disparity in sentencing between these two women justified a strong look and further investigation by the courts. I also emphasized that disparity is an important element that should have and could have been brought to the attention of the Supreme Court on a petition for writ of certiorari. I am critical of the public defender for not seeing that.

I noted that the majority criticizes my dissent for comparing Deegan's case to that of another North Dakota neonaticide. The majority asserts that almost nothing is known about the other North Dakota neonaticide that was committed by a North Dakota State University student.

True, the details underlying her crime are not part of the sentencing record. But an actual comparison of these women's circumstances, in light of Dr. Resnick's discussion of the § 3553(a) sentencing factors as related to neonaticide, strongly indicates that Deegan is entitled to a lenient sentence, similar to that of the NDSU student. And if the information before the judge and the testimony of Dr. Resnick was insufficient, it should have been a red flag to investigate further to determine whether the circumstances of the NDSU case were comparable to those of Deegan.

In any event, I said, what we do know about the other North Dakota neonaticide supports overturning Deegan's harsh sentence. Both women committed neonaticide. Both did so in North Dakota. But Deegan committed her crime on a reservation and landed in federal court.

As I have noted, Dr. Resnick reported that most women receive sentences of no longer than three years' incarceration, and the NDSU student received three years' probation. On the Deegan record, I asserted there is no just reason for the sentencing disparity between these two women. As I previously asked, what respect should be given to federal criminal law which imposed a harsh punishment for Deegan's crime committed on the reservation, when compared to the lenient sentence upon a woman off the reservation? Might an informed observer say: *just another injustice* by the United States that Indians must suffer?

The comparison of these two cases relates not to whether a federal court should rely on state sentences, but is an issue of unfairness and injustice to an Indian woman living on a reservation as compared to a woman not living on a reservation. The majority may say different laws apply. The difference here rests not on the law, but on the mistakes and misjudgment by a federal court as shown by the record.

I acknowledged that the case showed my sympathy and concern for Native Americans. I asserted that this country needs to re-evaluate its criminal justice system where, under the advisory guidelines, Indians often suffer heavier sentences than a counterpart prosecuted in a state court for a similar crime.

I wrote that I considered Deegan's sentence of ten years and one month to be very unfair and unjust. Native Americans and others need to ask the U.S. government to examine the great disparity in sentences between Native Americans sentenced by the federal government for crimes by Native Americans committed on an Indian reservation compared to the less harsh sentences for similar crimes committed off the reservation where state judges impose sentences under state law.

A constitutional issue of equal protection seemed to hit me between the eyes. Here's a quote from a letter Deegan's sister wrote to the sentencing judge:

> Non-Indian people may not easily internalize this sense of loss and powerlessness so deeply ingrained by American Indian people still today. The cultural deprivations and discriminations of our people merely because of our heritage have contributed to the psychological deficits that Dana, at that particular low time in her life, was unable to overcome. I fear that these same cultural factors may also contribute to harsher penalties of an already oppressed woman.

I thought this passage to be most appropriate in the circumstances. It constituted a brief and accurate portrayal of the manner that the federal courts treated or, shall I say, mistreated Dana Deegan — not really perceiving the injustice and unfairness of the more than ten-year prison sentence imposed in that case.[23]

— CHAPTER 31 —

James Dean Walker — Justice, Finally

This chapter recounts a remarkable story about doing justice under extraordinary circumstances and against the odds. It's a story of persistence resulting ultimately in the correction of a miscarriage of justice. Above all, it's a story of one judge's insistence that truth matters and that the rule of law requires that mistakes be acknowledged and rectified.

The case of James Dean Walker was a real-life experience for me. It probably is the most memorable case I have had among the 6,500-plus cases that I have sat on over the past years.

It started in the early morning hours of April 15, 1963, on a highway a couple of miles north of Little Rock, Arkansas, and it sounded like the ordinary criminal situation. Three people, James Dean Walker, his friend Russell Kumpe, and a lady friend, Linda Ford, had been in a bar drinking. One of them had a gun and the gun went off, so the three of them took off in an Oldsmobile. All seated in the front, Kumpe driving, Linda Ford in the middle and James Dean Walker in the passenger seat, they went speeding away out of Little Rock. The police followed and stopped them about two miles north of the city.

Walker was twenty-two years old and, by his own admission, he was in and out of trouble with the law. What happened has been the source of bitter contention over the past twenty years, but there are a few undisputable facts. Gunfire erupted, policeman Jerrell Vaughan of the North Little

Rock police force fell fatally wounded, and Walker himself was riddled with five bullet wounds.

Policeman Vaughan had gone to Walker's side of the car to find out what was going on. Another policeman by the name of Gene Barentine was at the rear of the car frisking Kumpe when the shooting started. Vaughan ended up dead outside the car and James Dean Walker was lying on the highway with bullets in his body.

A murder charge was brought against Walker after he recovered. It seemed like a pretty open-and-shut case. Linda Ford said Walker shot first and killed Officer Vaughan. The other testimony indicated that Officer Barentine was at the back of the car. While shooting through the back window, Barentine plugged Walker. The trial didn't take long. Walker's lawyer pleaded that Walker must have been insane to do what he did. The jury was out twelve minutes, the verdict was guilty, and it looked like a slam dunk (open-and-shut case). Walker received a death sentence.

On appeal, an Arkansas judge, Oscar Fendler, a lawyer appointed for a year to sit on the state Supreme Court, wrote the opinion and said, "Well, there's a lot of unusual evidence" and Walker received a new trial.

What do you know, Walker now had a second chance.

Several things started to unravel. First was a recovery of the bullets from Walker's body. They weren't from Barentine's gun. Those bullets came from Vaughan, the policeman who was killed. What did that mean? In the second trial, the state had to find a way to explain how, if Walker fired first, could Vaughan, with a bullet in his heart, then shoot Walker five times.

Second, Officer Barentine, who'd been shooting from the back of the car, had sawed off the barrel of his police gun before the trial. With a sawed-off barrel, it's almost impossible in a ballistics test to examine bullets to see if they fit that gun.

Third, Mary Roberts, a friend of Linda Ford, had come upon the scene in a taxi cab. Roberts wanted to testify this time that James Dean Walker never fired a shot.

Fourth, and more importantly, something happened between the first and second case that pervaded all the rest of the litigation: Walker had found religion and he wanted to be baptized. Three ministers from Little Rock went to the trial judge William Kirby and said, "Judge, can we take Walker out of jail and take him down to the church and baptize him?" The judge said to the sheriff, "Okay, you take James Dean Walker with the ministers and let him be baptized. If he tries to escape, shoot him dead! We are going to burn the S.O.B. anyway."

Fifth, a cab driver named Alderman had driven Mary Roberts and was following the Kumpe-Ford-Walker car. He was a witness who, in substance, gave a statement to the police. They never called him for the trial. He saw everything because the headlights of the police cars were on. According to Alderman, the only shooting came from Barentine and Vaughan. Walker lay prone outside the automobile when a shot rang out; Vaughan did a little dance, then fell dead.

After the second conviction, Walker became a born-again Christian. He was taken to several congregations to speak about what a bad guy he had been, but that he had found God and was reformed. He did well. He did so well, prison officials trusted him to go out to these congregations alone. But in 1975, Walker took off and went to California. The state of Arkansas finally found him in 1980 and asked that he be extradited. Walker objected.

Walker claimed that the Arkansas prison system was a very bad one and, therefore, he should not be extradited. The courts, including the U.S. Supreme Court, denied him relief. Walker again became an Arkansas prisoner, then serving his life sentence in solitary confinement.

Now the lawyers in Arkansas who took up Walker's case, without fee, filed a federal court lawsuit in Arkansas. When the federal district court gave Walker no relief, Walker appealed to the Court of Appeals for the Eighth Circuit before the panel of Judge Gerald Heaney, presiding, Judge Myron Bright and Judge Donald Ross.

My law clerk, Trish Maher, after spending weeks examining the record, comes to me and says, "Judge, I think Walker was framed."

Well, I couldn't believe that. I have heard it said that there are no cracks in the criminal justice system and I said to Trish, "It can't be."

For two weeks I spent every hour that I could reviewing more than many hundreds of pages in the record. When I got through reading it, I thought Walker needed justice. I called my friend Judge Gerald Heaney. "Jerry," I said, "I've just gone through this Walker record. This person is probably innocent." Judge Heaney had been on the prior case with Judges Floyd Gibson and Patrick Mehaffey in 1969 that had initially denied Walker relief on his first petition to the federal courts. Judge Heaney said to me, "It's one of the few cases in which I didn't examine the record," referring to the earlier federal case.

As panel members on the second or successive petition for writ of habeas corpus, the case before us, Judge Heaney and I wanted to grant relief, but Judge Ross did not. We faced a problem — should we grant relief as a panel or need we go to the full court for an en banc case? The reason we would need to go to the full court is that by granting relief, our panel majority decision (Judge Heaney and I) would be, in a sense, overruling a decision of a prior panel which denied the first appeal relating.

We decided to have the en banc court hear the second appeal. The en banc court initially intended to award Walker a new trial. But before the en banc opinion was filed, the court received two new judges appointed by President Reagan. Under an Eighth Circuit court rule that allowed any new judge to sit on an en banc case which was yet not final, we then heard the case over again (en banc with nine judges) and this time the two new judges voted against Walker, so it was now five-to-four against giving him any relief.

The last ruling was a blow.

A television news story reported that the Walker story might have ended in keeping him in prison if it weren't for recent publicity in Arkansas surrounding the case. An investigative reporter, Mike Masterson, uncovered disturbing new evidence, lending credence to the theory that Walker's companion, Russell Kumpe, might have killed Officer Vaughan. News reports also suggested that ballistics were badly mishandled and that Walker never fired a shot that night.

Let me summarize:

Kumpe's wife said to Masterson, "Kumpe told me that he killed Vaughan." There is evidence that Kumpe fired a shot and his wife says that he admitted killing Vaughan. Now, with new evidence, there was a petition for the court to take back the case and reconsider it. The Eighth Circuit took the case back for reconsideration and Judge Richard Arnold voted with the prior minority to make a new majority.

Judge Arnold said that he would have granted relief the first time, but not the second time. This time he said, "There's some new evidence, maybe Walker did have an unfair trial. Let's send it back and let a judge hear the evidence." So five-to-four, the Eighth Circuit returned the case to the district court.

A week before the hearing, reporter Masterson was following this case when a shocking revelation came to light. Paul McDonald with the Arkansas State Crime laboratory, who had been the ballistics officer for this case, was asked by the new prosecutor to go through his belongings and see if there was anything that the prosecutor should have on this case. McDonald found a transcript of a conversation between Kumpe and his sister that had been recorded in the jail. The recording contained the following statement by Kumpe:

> Now look, I am going to explain something to you. You understand that I did shoot at that policeman and he will go crazy trying to figure out what happened to the gun. If they place the gun in my hand, naturally they could, no they couldn't either, 'cause I had been back in his custody. I don't know what they could have done and at the time, I didn't care, for everyone was shooting at everyone else and I had some things on me that would have got me a hundred years. I had to get rid of them.

In addition to that passage in the transcript Kumpe added:

> Until he shot me, you don't know what happened over there. I do. The policeman committed suicide. He shot Walker first. See if you don't shoot Walker then we don't have all that trouble and he's still alive. What would you do if someone shot you first?

That was pretty strong stuff. But the federal district court was not convinced and denied Walker relief, and the case then comes up again before the Eighth Circuit. But the record contained all of this new testimony, Alderman's testimony and all of this stuff about Judge Kirby. But the main thing for Judge Arnold, who was the swing vote, is there is another person shooting. Maybe he shot too high, but the whole ballistics thing blew up and Judge Arnold said:

> I want you to know something. Everyone, every defendant is entitled to be tried before an unprejudiced judge. I didn't have enough before to give him successive habeas relief, which the rule says, in order to give habeas relief, among other things, it must be in the interest of justice. But now, there is enough to say Walker should have a new trial. The state had this statement of Kumpe, which indicated that

there was somebody else who might have killed Vaughan. That evidence has been suppressed and Walker is entitled to a new trial.

I wrote the new opinion. After twenty-two years together, Judge Ross, who was my antagonist but did not write the dissent, said, "I won't do anything more to stop you from giving Walker what he should get," although he still did not go along with me. So we granted Walker a new trial. I authored the new opinion just at the time I was taking senior status, June 1, 1985.

Walker continued to be free by pleading guilty to a lesser charge and received a sentence less than the time he had served in prison. Now he became a free man.

That was a tremendous case. Walker wrote me a letter like none other I had ever received. It is dated January 4, 1991, six years after the case had been decided by us. He wrote, in part:

> I have attempted numerous times to write this letter to you. Each time, never feeling that the letter adequately expressed my feelings. Perhaps I can do better this time. It is very difficult to know exactly how to express one's gratitude to a person who is largely responsible for saving your life. At the time I was on death row and during later years in Arkansas prison and especially after my capture from escape and extradition back to Arkansas and in those years of solitary confinement, I had no idea that a judge from Fargo, North Dakota, would be the person to become so offended by an injustice that occurred in Arkansas some 18 years earlier. I thank you for your integrity and for your willingness to fight to correct what you so aptly label a stain on our criminal justice system.

> I owe much to some fine and brilliant attorneys. I came through a very ugly ordeal gaining much more than was taken from me. I survived with most of my sanity and most of my health, and most of all, my dignity and self-respect. I thank you for allowing me to do so. In closing, I say thank you so very much for giving my life and freedom back to me. It is my prayer that your life may continue to be blessed in the most abundant ways.

I don't know anybody who can get any more pleasure than I did from feeling that there was a life saved. I have a piece of art in my office with the inscription that says, "Justice, Justice, Shall Thou Pursue, Deuteronomy 16:20." I have tried to follow that Biblical advice.

Walker calls me every year between Christmas and New Year's and wishes me happy holidays and remembers what I did for him. Incidentally, at my 45th anniversary as a federal judge, the program committee for the celebration brought Walker to Fargo and we met for the first time on July 27, 2013.

What does the tale of James Dean Walker mean to lawyers-to-be? It illustrates that the law is a wonderful profession and when the time comes that a lawyer can contribute to what the lawyer feels is justice, may the lawyer so contribute. Again, as William Cullen-Bryant wrote: "Truth crushed to earth will rise again.[24]"

— CHAPTER 32 —

Piper Kidnapping — Do What in Your Heart and Mind is Right

The philosophical statement used to title this chapter is derived from the July 27, 1972, kidnapping of Virginia Piper, one of the most famous or perhaps infamous criminal cases in Minnesota following World War II.

Here's the story of the kidnapping: Two masked, hooded men dressed in black invaded the Piper home and abducted Mrs. Piper. A ransom note left in the house demanded one million dollars in twenty-dollar bills for her return.

Handcuffed and forced to lie on the backseat of an automobile, Mrs. Piper became the unwilling companion of the kidnappers on their several-hour journey to a heavily wooded area of Jay Cooke State Park, a site in northeastern Minnesota near Duluth and one hundred forty miles north of Minneapolis. As they travelled, the kidnappers directed Mrs. Piper to tape record preliminary ransom delivery instructions.

Meanwhile, husband Harry Piper arranged for the delivery of the ransom. About 9:30 p.m. on Friday, July 28, he received a telephone call communicating his wife's tape-recorded message. He drove with the ransom money to a signpost in St. Louis Park, Minnesota. There he found a radio transmitter, which he placed on the dash of his car, and the first of a series of notes, which directed him on an intricate ransom run. During the course of the ransom money run, Mr. Piper removed the money from his car to a 1972 Chevrolet Monte Carlo as directed by the radio transmitter.

Ultimately, Mr. Piper abandoned the car at a Holiday Village Store in a suburb south of Minneapolis, where the FBI recovered the vehicle.

In the next five years, the FBI conducted an intensive investigation to apprehend the two kidnappers. Donald F. Larson and Kenneth James Callahan were investigated initially. Later, all of the investigation efforts concentrated on those two men. Finally on July 11, 1977, only a few weeks before the federal statute of limitations on kidnapping would expire, the government indicted the pair on the charge of kidnapping Mrs. Piper and transporting her by interstate commerce in violation of federal law.

After briefing, the panel on which I presided and included Judge Stephenson heard the case on June 12, 1978.

One of the issues on appeal focused on whether the district court had committed prejudicial error when Lynda Billstrom appeared as a witness after the parties had rested and the case was over as far as testimony was concerned and subject only to instructions and final argument. Our appeals panel remanded the case to the district court to hear and consider the Billstrom testimony. Chief Judge Edward Devitt's ruling on the remand order denying any relief dated September 1, 1978, was resubmitted to the same panel and the panel reached its decision on January 26, 1979.

I truly was troubled in my decision-making.

Here was the dilemma: Devitt, a judge with the highest credentials and one of the best regarded trial judges in this country, was also a good friend. I considered him to be a truly great district judge. I didn't like the idea of reversing him and I was hesitant to do so.

Moreover, the Piper kidnapping case was of great interest, particularly to the people of Minnesota, as well as to the nation. Two persons had been found guilty by a jury. Here I was thinking about setting aside that jury verdict and making this an unsolved case, at least if these two men were given a new trial. I sought some advice.

One of the great judges of America was Talbot Smith of Ann Arbor, Michigan. Judge Smith had been a Michigan Supreme Court justice, then a district judge in the district encompassing Detroit, and then had taken senior status in 1972. He had sat with the Eighth Circuit on many occasions since taking senior status. I had sat with him several times and I had the utmost respect for him.

I talked to Judge Smith on the telephone. The conversation went something like this:

Myron: "Talbot, I'm troubled. I have this very important case. It's important to the public, it's important to the litigants, it's important to the defendant, it's important to our court."

I explained the background of the case to him and mentioned particularly the remand order and the testimony of Lynda Billstrom. I also told him that I did not really want to reverse Devitt, a judge for whom I had the highest regard and respect. Here's what Talbot said in words that are engrained in my mind and memory even today:

"Myron, do what in your heart and mind is right."

I hung up the phone. I thought to myself, *do what in my heart and mind is right.*

I knew that in my heart and mind I should give Larson and Callahan a new trial and that I should give weight to the Billstrom testimony because, as I saw it, Billstrom's testimony would have made a big difference to a jury that had a difficult time with the evidence in this case.

The final decision, which I wrote, set aside the ruling of Chief Judge Devitt and the finding of guilt by the jury and ordered that Larson and Callahan be given a new trial. Judge Joe Ingraham agreed. Judge Roy Stephenson dissented.

In the second trial, the jury found Callahan and Larson not guilty.

I repeat a postscript, the philosophy given to me by Talbot Smith, which remains with me to this day: "Myron, do what in your heart and mind is right." I strive to follow it every day.[25]

— CHAPTER 32 —

Looking Back

At my age of ninety-four, of which sixty-six of those years represent my engagement in the law, twenty-one years as a lawyer followed by almost forty-five years as a federal judge, I ask myself: What have I done, what have I contributed to society in my work, particularly as a federal judge?

I am well aware that opinions of a federal circuit judge, for the most part, partake of a limited judicial life. Because literally thousands of legal opinions become published each year, the earlier works of a federal appellate judge for the most part fade into oblivion. Yet a few survive in one way or the other.

In my work, some of my memorable opinions became embodied in follow-up United States Supreme Court decisions and thus have a very long life. Among these I include *Green v. McDonnell Douglas*, discussed in chapter 27, and *Helm v. Solem*, discussed in chapter 26. I still take pride in a few other memorable cases that bear my name as author and did not reach a review status in the U.S. Supreme Court.

I particularly mention these cases discussed in separate chapters: *United States v. Dana Deegan*, chapter 30; *United States v. Robert Woosley*, chapter 24; *Vaughn v. United States*, chapter 23; *James Dean Walker v. A.L. Lockhart*, chapter 31; *Reserve Mining Co. v. United States*, chapter 25; *United States v. Larson and Callahan*, chapter 32.

I cannot guarantee the life and continuity of those opinions. But in my contributions to this country, I note the approximate one hundred young lawyers who have served as my law clerks. These men and women, most of them still practicing lawyers and a very few as judges, carry in their minds the imprint of my philosophy as a person and as a judge. Many have written of my influence upon their lives. These former law clerks, with whatever assistance I have been to them, will be positively contributing to a better life for themselves, their families and their clients in the active practice of law. Otherwise, their services and contributions will be made to others such as their employers, or, if in public service, then to the public.

I quote below from some of my former law clerks whose words are not atypical of the words that have come from other clerks:

> I could not have hoped for a better clerkship experience. You have been a true mentor and friend to me over the past year. We had some good times — from watching football games while you recovered from hip surgery to fishing and swimming as you regained your stride. I think we also did some good work together, which included injecting some common sense and compassion in the law on student loan forgiveness, recognizing that a war hero who served our country well did not get the same service in return when it came to his criminal trial, pushing a majority to limit its view on the scope of the Attorney General's discretion under the immigration statutes, gaining a unanimous panel for a new trial on what initially appeared a divisive issue of inconsistent jury verdicts, and reaching a judicious resolution of the controversial issue of discriminatory restrictions against nonresident access to sport hunting. I will remain forever grateful for the many lessons you taught me about life and the law. I know they will serve me well for many years.
>
> With the greatest appreciation,
> *James Sullivan* (Law Clerk 2005-2006)

When I accepted your offer to clerk in Fargo this year, I had no idea what a life-altering experience that decision would turn out to be. In fact, I would venture to say that I have gotten more out of my clerkship than any other clerk in the history of Judge Bright clerks. Thank you so much for giving me the opportunity to spend a year in Fargo and a year learning from you. It has truly changed my life.

>With fondest affection,
>Liisa Vehik *(Law* Clerk 2005-2006)

For Judge Bright, a better lawyer for having served you, a better man for having known you.

>*William Hannay III* (Law Clerk 1973-1974)

I cannot thank you enough for this experience. This clerkship has been an invaluable opportunity, and I will forever treasure the friendships I have made and all I have learned.

>*Aubrey Fiebelkorn-Zuger*
>(Law Clerk 2009-2011)

In so many ways, my clerkship with you is the job that keeps on giving. I am forever grateful. The clerkship was a great way to begin my career and, now, years later I am still benefitting from your support. Rest assured, I don't take it for granted and I will never forget it.

>*Matthew Anderson* (Law Clerk 1996-1997)

The clerkship was an exhilarating mix of research, writing, debate and camaraderie, and I have always considered it the real launching pad for my career. It was an honor and a privilege to have worked with you. Thank you again for your generosity and for putting your trust in a young law student from Georgetown.

>*Thomas Collin* (Law Clerk 1974-1975)

It has been my sincere honor and joy to work for you this year. I have learned invaluable insight into the judicial process, not to mention the law itself. You have been a wonderful mentor and good friend—not many clerks can say that the judge they admire is also their friend. Thank you for the opportunity, the companionship, and tutelage you gave me generously.

>*Caroline Hubbell Yingling*
>(Law Clerk 2006-2007)

Throughout the year you have been a consummate teacher and mentor, and a gracious host. It has been an honor to serve in your chambers.

Sterling P.A. Darling (Law Clerk 2006-2007)

I greatly value the time that I spent as your law clerk and consider you my greatest mentor. You had a tremendous influence on me.

Stephen G. Harvey (Law Clerk 1989-1990)

I count myself lucky to be one of those people whose lives you've touched. It is fair to say that my time with you changed the way I looked at both the law and concept of justice markedly and for the better.

Marc Kittner (Law Clerk 1981-1982)

These bright minds of the young people who served me as law clerks kept me alert and, if I may opine, thinking young. I acknowledge all of my clerks' great contributions and assistance to my work as a federal judge.

Acknowledgments

My law clerks and my staff, including my assistant for thirty years, Ms. Lana Schultz, as well as others who have worked for me, are part of my extended family. They have made my work and my life a real pleasure. I thank them all.

I cannot complete this process of looking back over my life without giving due credit to my late wife, Frances, better known as Fritzie. Her high ideals, her great intelligence and her wisdom in urging me to become a federal judge were wonderful influences in my life. I would say to her, "You made me what I am today. I hope you're satisfied."

Fritzie reveled in my being a judge. As a member of the court family, she extended the Brights' bonds of friendship to everyone with whom she came in contact — judges, spouses, staff, court employees, lawyers and law students. Without her, there would have been no judicial career, no teaching of law to students, lawyers or not-yet lawyers, and no warm friendships with almost everyone with whom we came in contact.

Yet, my full life wouldn't have been possible without the holders of my heart strings: my children, Joshua Bright and Dinah Golding; their spouses, Juli Bright and Christian Golding; my grandchildren, Amy Long, Sari Dickson and Adam Schultz; their father, Bill Schultz; along with their spouses, Jim Long, Brock Dickson and Kimberly Schultz; and my great-grandchildren, Will and Connor Long, Collins Dickson and Mason Myron Schultz. Each has given me the warmth of their love, young companionship, and a good reason to be a fine grandfather and great-grandfather.

I am a lucky person. I salute all of my extended family mentioned above and the wonderful friendships I have had in North Dakota, Minnesota and elsewhere in this country and other countries.

Myron H. Bright

Appendix
(Chapter 18)

Delegates to the Democratic Party convention in the spring of 1960 were:

John Murphy — my friend and a very dedicated party worker and the person who suggested that I support JFK for president in the forthcoming election; Angus Kennedy — I remember the name, he was a good worker, but I just cannot place him at this time; Irma Caliahan — a longtime Democratic Party worker, an Irish woman who was part of the Kelly clan that held the party together through the thin, earlier years; Lorraine Ignell — who had been county chairperson prior to me. She was the wife of a jeweler and a very intelligent and hard-working Democrat; Henry Youngberg — I do not recollect this person; Orly Nelson — I recall the name, but I cannot recall the person; Jerome Shermoen — Jerry, as we called him, was a young lawyer in Fargo, the son of a railroad worker, a longtime friend and a candidate for the Legislature in the Fargo at-large district. He lost but he was a good worker. Jerome and I have been friends all of our lives; William Clower — Bill and his wife were strong Democratic workers. Bill was a teamster and, as I recall, was employed by one of the businesses in Fargo; Wallace Kapaun — one of the members of my group leading the party from 1958-1960. He was a local businessman and an able, dedicated person; Helen Pepple — a neighbor of Quentin Burdick's, a good friend, an intelligent person and a strong supporter of Burdick. She was named, I think, treasurer of the Quentin Burdick Organization when he ran for the Senate; Phyllis Hunter — the wife of a prominent Fargo physician. We did not have very many doctors in Fargo who supported the Democratic Party, but her husband, G. Wilson Hunter, was one of them. Phyllis and her husband had a very large home and entertained Fargo Democratic Party functions. In particular, she was the hostess following the Burdick birthday party and provided food and sustenance for JFK and his party and those persons who were involved in the program that Sunday, June 19th; Sharon Palon — Sharon was a friend of Helen Pepple, lived in the same neighborhood and worked with her friends; Marguret Svabodny — a strong precinct committeeperson who worked with me on party matters over the years; A.O. Kunert — chairman of the Nonpartisan League. He was very helpful in making sure that the Cass County Nonpartisan League supported Burdick for the Senate in its NPL convention; H.A. Halgrimson—a local attorney and insurance adjustor and a very devoted and dedicated Democrat; Barbara Lindell—who, along with Helen Pepple and Phyllis Hunter, were three women who were very strong, active workers in the party. Barbara was a bright lady who could stand up and debate with the best of them; Horace Rairdon—a party worker who I recall was very active in the labor movement; Vivian Steedsman—also a party worker who was in the labor movement; Nellie Thompson—worked with the labor movement and was a strong supporter of Democratic Party politics; Mike Dobervich—who had a tremendous World War II record. He was involved with his brother in the manufacturing of jam and jelly and he and his wife were strong supporters of the party; W.W. Murray—president of the AFL-CIO in North Dakota and, of course, supported Democratic candidates; Helen Ginakes—the wife of Connie Ginakes, who operated a restaurant in Fargo. The Ginakeses provided funds, support and even food for our Democratic meetings; E.F. Mertens—an official in the Teamsters Union and a strong supporter of Quentin and other Democratic candidates; P.W. "Bill" Lanier Jr., one of the outstanding lawyers in Fargo and one of the strongest Democrats in North Dakota. His family came from Tennessee and Bill grew up in Jamestown. He possessed great ability as a lawyer, as a speechmaker and as a Democratic politician. In later years, he ran for the U. S. Senate as an endorsed candidate of a Democratic Party and he served as the state party chairman; Joe Poer—my neighbor, my right-hand person in the Democratic Party and in my work for Quentin in 1960. He was a truck driver, a member of the Teamsters Union who did whatever I asked him to do. He helped very much in looking after JFK when JFK had come to the birthday party; Larry Hunter—a business man in Fargo and a good supporter; George Krueger—also a Teamster, an official in a Nonpartisan League, and a great supporter of Democratic causes; Richard Blair—Richard was a young man in Fargo. He had political ambitions and he supported our party; Abner Moberg—also a businessman in Fargo and a good supporter; John Casper—a hard worker in the party; Margaret Waxler—When I mention Margaret, I also again include Joe Poer because those two people worked so closely with me in all party matters. Margaret worked in Democratic headquarters and served as the secretary of the party, doing the work that had to be done to maintain an office and to promote the party. I give so much credit to both Margaret and Joe Poer for the success of the Democratic Party in Cass County in 1960; Myron Bright — I will not say anything more here about myself; Bernard Majors — a strong Democratic worker and insurance agent and a person who was interested in politics and served the cause well; Rep. Quentin Burdick — the man we wanted to elect to the U.S. Senate; Ethel Warner — a good friend who served as a secretary of the party; Joe LaValley — a party worker who I cannot recall particularly; Milton Bergseth — a local optometrist and a silent force in the business community supporting the Democrats; Catherine Swanston — an older lady and the widow of a very prominent North Dakota businessman who had been in the automobile business. Her roots were Irish and they went back to the early days of politics in North Dakota. We were pleased to have her participation in the convention; J. G. Page — an elderly, but a strong supporter.

Ninth District alternates included:
Mrs. Curtis G. Olson — wife of my successor as county chairperson; Mrs. Bernard Majors — a strong supporter; Mrs. Mike Dobervich — Mrs. Dobervich and her husband were strong supporters. The wives of the men mentioned, for the most part, participated and were strong supporters; Frank Knox — Frank and I were close friends. He was a lawyer in Fargo and a former FBI agent. He and I had attended law school at the University of Minnesota together and was right there whenever I needed assistance on party matters. He was one of the best and greatest Democrats that I ever had anything to do with. He was a law partner with Bill Lanier; Mrs. E. F. Merlens; Mrs. George Krueger; and, of course, my wife Fritzie, whom I have mentioned as part of the team many times. Others were Mrs. Virginia Jensen — a school teacher and former chair of the Democratic Party and a strong supporter; Stella Staska — the wife of a local architect and also a supporter; Rosemary Murphy — I have mentioned her husband, John; Mrs. Richard Boulger — a strong Democrat, as was her husband, who happened to be an assistant U.S. attorney and thus could not personally be involved in politics; Myron Hovden — a local man who was interested in politics.

The Tenth District included part of rural Cass County and had six delegates with a full vote each. They included:
Fred Backstrand — a farmer from Kindred and a strong supporter;

Guy Hildreth — a strong supporter from Argusville; Ed Nesemeier, Casselton — he operated a large farm near Casselton and had run for office on the Democratic ticket in years past; E.J. Morton of Horace — I cannot remember him particularly; John Yunker, Durbin — a farmer in that area who served in the state Senate for many years; Aaron Andre, Mapleton — a hard worker for the Democratic Party.

Tenth District alternates were:

J. Milton Myhre, Casselton, a member of the House; Irwin Trana and Harold Trana, both from Kindred. Others alternates were George Sinner, a young farmer from Casselton who later became one of the outstanding North Dakota governors; Mrs. John Yunker, Durbin, a strong supporter of our party and a strong supporter of her husband who ran for political office; and Roy Krajeck, a businessman in southwest Fargo and chairman of the Democratic precinct committeeman from that area.

Eleventh District — ten delegates with a half vote each:

Nick Brown of Leonard; Earl Maker of Hunter — an early supporter of Burdick, both for the U.S. House of Representatives and also for the Senate and, as I remember, he was one of those who was named on the B for Burdick Committee; John Toussaint, Leonard; Bruce Brewer, Erie; Randolph Moen, Hunter; Mrs. Ed Powers, Leonard, was a very active worker and later became a member of the Legislature; Albin Olson, Argusville; Henry Wolf, Leonard; Robert Locket, Wheatland, who, became my very good friend and was one of the most dedicated party workers we had, a particularly close friend of Bill Guy; William Merlin, Chaffee.

Eleventh District alternates:

Mrs. O.H. Trapp of Enderlin; A.J. Kapaun, Alice; Mrs. Fred Thompson, Casselton — one of the most active workers in that area; Joe Schafer, Amenia; R.C. Bartholomay, Wheatland.

Notes

[1] The spelling may properly be Kagarlyk, Ukraine.

[2] I entered a Keds (tennis shoes) slogan contest. My entry, "Keds never slip, always grip," made me the Minnesota state winner of a dog or bicycle. I took the bicycle.

[3] A "Dear John" letter is one where the soldier's sweetheart who remains in the United States writes her soldier or sailor and says, in effect, "I've found another guy and our romance is over. Goodbye and good luck." This rejection often occurred, as it did with me when Harriet wrote me that she was about to marry a former boyfriend from Omaha, who, coincidentally, had just returned from military service in India, where I was then stationed. For a second time, Myron said sadly to himself, "Goodbye, Harriet, sweetheart."

[4] *United States v. Norris*, (8th Cir. 2006), reversed and remanded, (2007)

[5] *State v. Broadway Investment Co.* (North Dakota 1957)

[6] *State v Guy* 1961

[7] *Merchants National Bank and Trust Company, as administrator and Personal Representative of the Estate of Eloise A. Newgard, deceased v. United States*, United States District Court for the District of North Dakota (1967)

[8] *United States of America v Irvin Warfield, Jr.* (1966)

[9] *Vaughn v. United States*, 404 F.2d 586 (8th Cir. 1968)

[10] *Woosley v. United States*, 478 F.2d 139 (8th Cir. 1973)

[11] 83 Minn.L.Rev. at 299, 302 (Dec. 1998)

[12] *Reserve Mining Co. v. EPA*, 514 F.2d 492 (8th Cir. 1975)

[13] *Helm v. Solem*, 684 F.2d 582 (8th Circuit 1982)

[14] *Green v. McDonnell Douglas Corp.*, 463 F.2d 337 (8th Circuit 1972)

[15] Attorney General Eric Holder Delivers Remarks at the Annual Meeting of the American Bar Association's House of Delegates, www.justice.gov/iso/opa/ag/speeches/2013/ag-speech-130812.html

[16] *United States v. O'Meara*, 895 F.2d 1216, 1221 (8th Cir. 1990) (Bright, J., dissenting)

[17] *United States v. Hiveley*, 61 F.3d 1358, 1363 (8th Cir. 1995) (Bright, J., concurring)

[18] *United States v. England*, 966 F.2d 403, 411 (8th Cir. 1992) (Bright, J., concurring)

[19] See *United States v. Loaiza-Sanchez*, 622 F.3d 939, 942 (8th Cir. 2010) (Bright, J., dissenting)

[20] *United States v. Hiveley*, 61 F.3d 1358, 1364 (8th Cir. 1995) (Bright, J., concurring)

[21] I use the term "rose-colored glasses" to indicate judges do look at facts colored by their own life's experiences affecting a judicial philosophy of a judge. My life's experiences are very different from my much younger colleagues.

[22] *United States v. Tom*, (2007)

[23] *United States v. Deegan*, 605 F.3d 625 (8th Circuit 2010)

[24] *Walker v. Lockhart*, 763 F.2d 942 (8thh Circuit 1985)

[25] *United States v. Larson and Callahan*, 596 F.2d 759 (8th Circuit 1979)

INDEX

Alito Jr., Sam 135
Anderson, Kenneth 55
Anderson, Matthew 173
Anderson v. Schreiner 55, 56
Arnold, Richard 164

Barentine, Gene 162
Bearman, M.L. "Bill" vii, viii, 64
Benson, Asmunder 49
Billstrom, Lynda 169, 170
Blackmun, Harry 120
Brand, Irving 13, 14
Bright, Frances "Fritzie" Reisler ii-iii, v-viii, 35, 37, 38, 40, 42-44, 48-49, 51, 62-71, 73-74, 78, 81-83, 85, 87- 88, 92-93, 96-99, 101, 103-104, 106, 109, 111-119, 126, 135, 175, 179, Photo pages 3, 6
Bright, Hinda "Ann" 1
Bright, Joseph 4, 8-9, 11, 18-19, 25, Photo page 7
Bright, Joshua 51, 175, Photo page 8
Bright, Dina (Golding) 51, 108-109, 175, Photo page 8
Bright, Lena ix, 1, 3,-6, 8-10, Photo pages 2, 4
Bright, Leo 4, 9-10, 120, Photo page 7
Bright, Mabel 4, 9-10, 120, Photo page 4
Bright, Morris ix, 1-6, 8-9, Photo page 2
Bright, Nochim "Sam" 1-2, 5
Bright, Rochelle George 8-9, 18, 25, 120
Bright, Roy 4-5, 9-10, 18-19, 120, Photo page 7
Brink, David 13-14, 37-38
Broadway Investment Company 53
Burdick, Eugene ii, 79, 88, 104-105, 107

Burdick children, Jessica, Jan, Jon, Jennifer 78, 80
Burdick, Jocelyn ii, 62, 72-73, 93, 98-99
Burdick, Marietta 62-64, 78
Burdick, Quentin ii, v, vii, 51, 62-63, 65, 67-68, 70, 72-73, 76, 78-79, 81, 83-89, 91, 93-94, 97-99, 103-109, 115, 118, 177-179, Photo pages 5, 6
Burdick, Usher 67, 70, 72, 79, 106, 114, 116
Burger, Warren 128, 133, 144

Callahan, Kenneth 169-171
Camp Lee 21-25
Christopher, Warren 113
Cohen, Roger 56
Collin, Thomas 173
Conrad, Kent 98-100
Cordero, Colonel 26, 32-33

Darling, Sterling 174
Davies, Ronald 58, 107, 121, 147-148
Davis, John 73, 78, 87, 89-90, 92-93
Deegan, Dana 146, 153-159, 160, 171
Deegan v. United States 142, 153, 157, 171
Devitt, Edward 120, 169-170
Dick, Lawrence 54
Dick v. New York Life Insurance Company 53
Dobervich, Eli and June 73
Dorgan, Byron 99

Erickson, Larry 114, 116
Evans & Novak 111
Eveleth (Minn.) viii, 4-11, 19, 21-23, 25, 29, 36-37, 40, 42-43, 61, 130

Fair Store 6, 9
Farber, Daniel 131
Fargo Forum 49, 70, 82-83, 93, 97, 112-113

Fendler, Oscar 162
Fiebelkorn-Zuger, Aubrey 173
Fitch, Ken 92
Fort Crook 24-25
Fort Snelling 19
Fraser, Everett 13, 42-43
Freeman, Orville viii, 14, 37, 81, 81
Frey, Andrew 145

Gibson, Floyd R. 123-125, 163
Gilbert (Minn.) 4-6, 9-10, 130
Ginsburg, Ruth Bader 150, back cover, Photo page 8
Golding, Chris 175, Photo page 8
Graham v. Florida 135-136
Green, Percy 137-141
Green v. McDonnell Douglas 137-141, 171
Guy, Jean 73-74
Guy, William L. "Bill" ii, viii, 57, 72-74, 76-77, 80, 91, 97, 101-102, 104, 108, Photo page 6

Hannay, William III 173
Harvey, Stephen 174
Hawkins, Margaret Benson 49
Heaney, Gerald 120
Helm v. Solem 133, 135-136, 171
Heuther, William 66
Hodges, Luther 97
"Hucka" 9-10
Humphrey, Hubert ii, x, 70, 74, 80, 102, 106
Hunter, G. Wilson 84-86, 91, 177
Hunter, Phyllis 91, 177-178

Iron Range (Minn.) i, viii, ix, 4-5, 7, 11, 15, 17, 21-22, 36, 41, 61, 73, 102, 132

Jaffe, Morrie 15
Johnsen, Harvey 139
Johnson, Lyndon ii-iii, v, viii, ix-xi, 74, 80, 102, 104-106, 111-113, 119, Photo page 6
Jones, James ix-x, 115-116

Kefauver, Estes 71

Kelly, David 62
Kelly, Dennis 120, back cover
Kennedy, John "Jack" ii, viii, 66, 74-76, 79-86, 104, 108-109, Photo page 5
Kennedy, Robert "Bobby" ii, x, 107-111
Knox, Frank 58-59, 70, 84, 179
Kumpe, Russell 161-165

Ladin, Harold 17
Langer, William "Bill" 71-72, 97
Lanier, P.W. "Bill" Jr. 62, 69, 76, 78, 83, 178-179, Photo page 6
Larson, Donald 169-171
Lashkowitz, Herschel 66, 73, 97
Lay, Donald 139, 163
Levant, Maurice "Muck" 61
Lewis and Hammer 41-42
Lindell, Wallace 82
Lord, Miles 129

Maher, Trish 163
Manfield, Harry 9, 120
Marks, Myron "Mike" 22
Maslon, Samuel 41
Masterson, Mike 164
Matthes, M.C. 123-125, 129
McDonald, Paul 165
McGovern, George ii, 82, 109, 111
McKinley (Minn.) 4, 6
Minnesota Law Review 14, 16-17, 37, 131
Murphy, John 74, 78, 81, 83, 86, 88, 90, 92, 104, 177, Photo page 5
Murphy, Rosemary 78, 81, 93, 179
Murray, Bill 106
Mussman, William 14, 38

Newgard, William Bry 57
Newman, Harriet 24-25
Nilles, Oehlert and Nilles 52, 58-59
Nixon, Richard 73, 78, 80, 86-87, 144

Oehlert, Lewis 52, 58-59
Olson, Curtis 69, 96
O'Meara v. Kost 149, 151

Pepple, Gordon 63
Pepple, Helen 63, 65-66, 70, 177-178
Perlman 28
Piper, Harry 168-169
Piper, Virginia ii, 168-169
Powell 134-135, 141
Poyzer, Floyd 102
Pundt, Lyle 66

Register, George 120, Photo page 7
Reisenfeldt, Stephen 38
Reserve Mining Company ii, 129, 131
Resnick, Philip 156-158
Rockefeller, Nelson 78
Ross, Donald 129-130, 139-141, 163-164, 166

Schreiner, Alfred 55-56
Shamshernagar 29-30, 32
Shriver, Sargent 81-82
Silver, Betty 16-17, 19-21, 23-24
Simon, Kenneth 36, 38
Sinner, George "Bud" 98-100, 107
Smelcer, Nonee 24
Smith, Steve 82
Smith, Talbot 169-170
Sotomayor, Sonia 135
Stevenson, Adlai 74
Sullivan, James 172
Sweeney, Eugene 94
Symington, Stuart 74, 80, 82-84, 86, 88

Teigen, Obert 120
Temple, Larry ix, 115
Tighe, Charles 77, Photo page 6
Truman, Harry ii
United States v. Booker 148-150
United States v. Deegan 157
United States v. England 151
United States v. Hiveley 150-151
United States v. Norris 28

Vaughan, Jerrell 127, 161-164, 166
Vaughn v. United States 123, 148, 171
Vehik, Liisa 173
Vogel, Charles 104-105, 111, 120, Photo page 7
Vogel, Mart 42-43, 47, 52, 57, 62-63, 65-66, 95, 103-104, 106
Vogel, Philip 43-45, 51, 53-55, 62-63, 66, 95, 103-104, 106

Walker, James Dean 161-167, 171, Photo page 8
Warfield, Irwin 58
Wattam, Charles 43, 45, 106
Welsh v. United States 125
White, Byron 113
White House ii-iii, v-vi, ix-x, 109, 111, 114-119
Wilk, Mort 95
Woosley v. United States 126-128, 171

Yingling, Caroline 173
Young, Milton ii, 105-106, 76